CLAIM YOUR PAIN
RESCUE YOUR DREAMS

HOPE
CHANGES
EVERYTHING

LANCE LANG

Published by:

the
treehouse
group, llc

P.O. Box 1301, Harrisburg, NC 28075
thgroup.net

ISBN: 978-0-9903118-0-5
Printed in the United States of America
Library of Congress Cataloging-in-Publication Data

For information regarding author interviews or speaking engagements, please contact the public relations department – Lance@LanceLang.com.

What's being said about
Hope Changes Everything

"Lance Lang does not sugar-coat the suffering nor does he look through a 'rose-colored glass' at the reward. This is a no nonsense, straight-shooting, hard-hitting, Christ-centered, and life-proven testimony of one man's journey which in so many ways mirrors every person's struggle. It is a great guide for those who do not want to allow pain and suffering to triumph over them any longer!"

-Nick Garland, Pastor First Baptist Church Broken Arrow

"Here's why I like Lance Lang: He shares his poverty. He's honest and vulnerable and authentic. He's a great listener. He really cares about people. He's been through it. But the big, big thing is - he's a hope dealer. He recognizes suffering and pain, but he also believes that hope, joy, and grace transform people. That's a powerful thing. I need it."

-Doug Serven, Pastor City Presbyterian Church, Oklahoma City

"God has uniquely equipped Lance Lang. He has used the fire of pain to forge a heart of gold and a message. That message is razor sharp; but the cut is like a surgeon's, purposed to heal. May the Lord use this book to encourage you and give you hope."

-Dr. Hance Dilbeck, Pastor Quail Springs Baptist Church, Oklahoma City

"I encourage you to grab several copies of *Hope Changes Everything* and begin to share them with those individuals you know who are struggling with life. We all need a little hope; thanks to Lance for shining light on where to find it."

-Gregory "Heady" Coleman, Pastor North Church, Oklahoma City

"The transparency of Lance's writing is so refreshing! And although we may not know all the answers this side of eternity when it comes to pain, reading this book will give you hope and assurance that God is with you in the midst of it all."

-Ronnie Baker II, Founding and Lead Pastor of Audacity Church, Tulsa

"Lance Lang knows pain. This book is compelling, convincing, insightful, and edgy. If you or someone you care about is facing pain caused by addiction, this read might be the difference between hopelessness and hope."

-Dr. David Willets, Author of *Silverlining: A Life Application Journey Through the Dynamics of Grief*

"Lance relates how our pain tries to redefine us. Whether the pain is from addiction, failures, or abuse, we see through Lance's own life that hope changes everything. This book caused me to consider my own pain and remember the undeserving hope I have in Jesus."

-Cameron Whaley, Pastor Canadian Valley Baptist Church, Yukon

"Lance has struck a chord that will resonate in the hearts of those who read this book. His story is a living testimony to the truth that God is able to transform your pain to victory and hope. You will be encouraged by the hope of Jesus as you read."

-Dr. Brian Pain, Pastor First Baptist Duncan

For Mom & Dad,

Because you stood in the gap for me,

I can now stand in the gap for others.

Your mission is accomplished.

I Love you.

CONTENTS

FOREWORD

I was hopelessly lost. While visiting a large city in a foreign country, I went out for a walk one evening to take in the sights and sounds, to see the life and experience the energy of the culture and find some food, much of which was cooked and served in local neighborhood booths. The air was filled with local music emanating from speakers propped on balconies of second-story cafes. With each turn down a different street, there were new beats and new aromas of food.

The streets eventually turned to cobbled stone and every alley was lined with shoppers and vendors selling all types of clothing and trinkets. There was life on every street, couples sat at tables for two, families dinning together while communities of friends stood and chatted.

All my senses were engaged in the moment, to the point where I lost track of time and I lost track of my bearings.

I had no idea how many streets I'd wandered down or what any of those street names were. I was in a part of town I knew nothing of, in a city whose language I didn't speak. And to make things worse, I'd even been totally abandoned by Google maps!

Like I said: I was lost.

As I absorbed my condition, the sounds of people and cars swirling around me started making me panic. My outing of joy now felt more like desperation, and so I did what anybody would do in my position—I stopped a few people on the street, made big hand gestures, and slowly yelled words at them in English (*"Where hotel?! English?!"*) as though that would help. I wandered those streets looking for some sign of hope that I could find my way back, looking for someone who could at least give me a clue to get back home.

I stumbled in to a local market populated by people buying fresh produce. I stepped a few feet inside the store and yelled, *"English anyone?!"*

A college student spoke up. "Yes, I do," he said.

You can't imagine my relief.

I couldn't remember the name of my hotel, so I launched into describing the building. He listened, then drew a map on the back of his grocery receipt and pointed me in the right direction. I looked at his drawing, which showed two left turns, a zigzag, and then a right turn. For me, it wasn't much of a map.

He must've seen the confusion in my eyes, because he graciously said, "I'll guide you there," and off we went.

Except I didn't recognize *anything*, so I kept saying, "I don't remember this. Are you sure we're going the right way?" Up the streets, through alleyways, step after step, I was in such a frazzled emotional state that I nervously second-guessed his route. "Wait! I think we should be over there!"

Until it occurred to me that, if I was going to get back to my hotel that night, I knew I had to let go. I was going to have to abandon my attempts to control the journey and trust my guide. *which is for me my hard lesson*

Lance Lang is a guide who knows his way through the shabby streets of the soul, littered with debris of vanity, secrets, and broken dreams. To those who have lost their hope and dreams, who have taken an indiscriminate beat-down from pain, there is a guide to navigate you through this garbage of illusions and delusions, someone who knows how to draw a map of the way back, and more importantly someone who knows a way out from all the vacant images, empty of the promise they once held.

You are not alone in your journey. There is a guide to help find a message in the mess.

Lance has been there.

What you'll find with in the pages of this book are the words of a compassionate guide. Because Lance has known the honesty and mercy of Jesus, Himself the ultimate compassionate guide. Like my foreign guide, Lance is a man who has been down all the alleys, who knows from experience which ones that don't lead anywhere. In this book, Lance volunteers to travel alongside you and show you the way to hope.

Lance has experiential knowledge of the pain and the healing. He has walked through the streets of his pain with the One who heals; those like Lance who have found and fed on the ministry of Jesus are more able to commit themselves to guiding others into freedom, unafraid to confront the opposing forces of addiction. People who have been restored in a particular area of pain have a special gift to minister to others with similar problems, perhaps because they've encountered and experienced the power of God's healing presence.

As you enter the pages of this book you might find your struggles are different from Lance's. That's fine. Because this book confronts the major war each of us must fight in order to win the battle with pain. The war of hope.

There are not many good things associated with the word "dealer." There are car dealers, drug dealers, card dealers, and wheeler-dealers... and Lance has been them all. But today he's a new kind of dealer: a hope dealer, seeking to inject others with the power of hope. Here in this book he deals out hope in mega doses.

The one element that will change every situation is hope. How to find real, lasting hope when the dream has died is the focus of this book. Hope helps. It pulls freedom out of despair, wholeness out of brokenness, vision out of darkness, and life out of death. This is not a book of quick-fix solutions; it's an entrance into a steady journey from hopelessness to hope.

To find freedom there first must be faith, and to have faith there first must be hope. Hope is a hinge on which a life of freedom swings.

There's good news for the burned-out, beaten, and defeated, and the more desperate the situation, the stronger the hope. We can't live without hope, it pushes our perceived limits of what we thought was ever possible. Hope is how we get from one day to the next. To have hope is to believe it's worth taking the next step; that our lives, families, and actions are worth living for. It's hope that gives us energy to keep going day after day. Hope hollers at us, "There is a way out! It doesn't have to be this way!" even from the most dangerous and depressing situations.

The places of pain can become the palaces where hope is revealed or, as Lance perfectly describes, "your pain can become your platform." Hope has the power to gather the fragments of life-devastating decisions, and shattered dreams, by bringing us In contact with Jesus, the One who guides us into life as it was meant to be.

Hope will get you home.

Hope changes everything.

– David Edwards, Oklahoma City, OK

March 2014

INTRODUCTION

"Saddle up your horses; we've got a trail to blaze.

Through the wild blue yonder of God's amazing grace."

These are the epic opening lyrics to the corny Steven

Curtis Chapman song entitled "The Great Adventure." It's

cheesy and full of over-the-top backup vocals, but the lyrics still

ring true – regardless of the hairstyle of the lead singer.

The song says this:

> *Come on, get ready for the ride of your life*
>
> *Gonna leave long-faced religion in a cloud of*
>
> *dust behind*
>
> *And discover all the new horizons just waiting*
>
> *to be explored*
>
> *This is what we were created for*

Saddle up your horses; we've got a trail to blaze

Through the wild blue yonder of God's amazing grace

Let's follow our leader into the glorious unknown

This is a life like no other – this is The Great Adventure

This is so true. I love it! "A life like no other." Doesn't that sound *good*? It does to me. Today I feel like I live a Great Adventure-style life. A life so far past anything I could have ever dreamed I could live. And you know what? It has *nothing* to do with money, status or success and *everything* to do with fully accepting my purpose and my pain.

This is the life I believe we are all called to live! When we fully embrace grace and fully release our guilt, then we're embarking on a great adventure that will take us to places we only dreamed we could experience. It will place us perfectly in the path of a stranger who needs just what we can offer. It will give us talents we can use so effortlessly people will think we're part alien. When you find yourself in the middle of God's great adventure of grace, you'll feel like you're dreaming a dream so pure and perfect it could only come from a perfect Creator.

The adventure of grace is where we belong. It fits around us like a perfectly stitched set of footie pajamas. You slide into it and life just seems to make sense around you. Ego and pride seem meaningless, worry and doubt seem like wastes of time, and the solitude you used to despise becomes a welcome home. When you step into the grace of Jesus Christ, the world begins to make a lot more sense. Your life begins to make more sense; your past begins to make more sense.

Your pain will begin to make more sense.

Yes. I said *pain*.

How can a great life – one that makes perfect sense, that is filled with meaningful and significant relationships, that basically fits like a glove – have *anything* to do with pain?

For starters, pain is a universal affliction no human is privileged enough to escape. Every person who has taken even a brief tour on this planet has experienced pain at some point, and until we pass away, we will continue to experience it. We cannot escape pain. We can't run from it, pay it off, ignore it, move away from it, yell at it until it cowers in submission, shop it away, drink it away, snort it away, eat it away, or push it away. Pain hits all of us. For most people, it hits us hard, it hits us early, and it keeps on hitting.

As children, each of us had a dream. You did. I did. We all did. A dream of the perfect life. We specifically imagined this idealized life to fulfill the definition of success, happiness and *perfection* for us. Some would be this, some would be that. Some would go here, some would go there. But no matter where we went or what we did, it would all be perfect. Right? Life before the pain was a dream, a dream we all had.

So what happened? Where did it go? Why didn't it happen? What's wrong with us that caused the dream to fade? Is it something we did? Is it something someone else did? Did anything really ever happen at all?

For many of us, somewhere along the way, our dreams seemed to slip out of our grasp. We watched as they slid inch-by-inch out of our hands as the pain of a broken/lost/hurtful relationship, the agony of an unexpected tragedy, or the guilt of a mistake pushed us off balance. We tried to maintain our focus, believing that maybe the dream was still possible. But doubts built day by untreated day and soon the pain overcame the promise of a dream fulfilled.

Unfortunately, life is not a choose-your-own-adventure book. When the thorn of disappointment, abuse, or manipulation pricks our skin, we don't have the option to flip back a few pages and choose a different outcome. We don't have the privilege of changing the pain of the past.

In whatever form you've experienced it, when pain pricks you, it makes its way into your proverbial blood stream. If left unaddressed, that pain will slowly change you day by day, altering everything about the way you live. How you view those around you. How you react. How you think. How you speak. How you treat others. Your ability to be a friend, be a parent, be a son or a daughter. It changes your mood, your relationship with God, even your thoughts about eternity.

Pain changes everything about you.

When we got hurt, we got changed.

Most people walk through life never understanding what happened. How the dream slipped away. Why they feel so angry inside. Why they make fun of others. Why they ridicule and mock people in their minds. Why they can't seem to sustain a relationship. Why they can't shake insecurity. Why they always feel like they're unwanted. Undesired. Undeserving.

Pain is the ultimate creeper. It sticks with us, slowly changing us little by little each day. It's not like we get hurt and instantly become different people. Even those who have experienced the most tragic of circumstances say that the weight of guilt and shame built up day after day, month after month, year after year, until they couldn't take it any more and they snapped.

Over the past several years, as I've journeyed through my own personal battle with pain and walked alongside hundreds of others, I've seen a theme in those who find a way to overcome and those who don't. For the latter, it sucks. I hate it. I can't stand to see someone hurting and feel useless. I want to put my hands on their shoulders and just scream, *It doesn't have to be this way! There is hope! You can have your dream back!* Sometimes I feel like I want it for them more than they do.

But that's just the power of pain. It drives you to be apathetic, lies to you about who you really are and what you're actually capable of. It pushes you farther and farther away from who you were originally created to be.

In this book you'll journey through my deepest and darkest experiences with pain. It won't all be pretty, but it will all be real. Sometimes it's hard to be completely honest and vulnerable, but I've chosen to go there in hopes that it may give you the permission you need to go there as well, to dive into the pain, to wrestle with it, to name it, to claim it, and ultimately to get rid of it. To see yourself as God sees you: the perfect creation He formed together. To begin to find ways to manage the feelings that will arise on your way back from pain. I want you to put this book down with a confidence that pops your head up, pushes your shoulders back, and puts a swagger in your step that causes people to say, *What happened to them?!* I want you to come away with a self-realization like never before, feeling powerful and vulnerable enough to accept the baggage of your past, to forgive all of those who've hurt you, and most importantly to begin to form a love for yourself like never before.

Hope comes to those who are willing to take a risk and try something new, even if it might hurt a little. But to get to somewhere we've never been, we must be willing to do some things we've never done. Do you want a hope that will never leave you? Do you want the dream life you've always desired?

I hope so. Because hope changes everything.

CHAPTER 1

DREAMS WE ONCE HAD

As is often the case with so many stories, mine starts with a dream.

When I was in the formative stages of my adolescence, I had a dream. Of course, most kids at that age have multiple dreams for their future, often ones that an adult would understand as competing with one another. Kids, though, in that marvelous way that kids have, can turn those competing dreams into something that makes sense. In a kid's mind, being a punk rock star goes completely with being a scientist, which also goes with being an arctic explorer. Sure, of course you can do all three. Why not?

I wanted to do a lot of different things when I was a

kid, but again and again I came back to one specific dream. I guess you could call it my dream of all dreams: I wanted to be a politician. I didn't want to be the President of the United States – I just wanted to be a congressman. Serving in the House of Representatives or the Senate, with my beautiful, adoring, vibrant wife and my three healthy, bright-smiling, well-behaved children by my side at campaign events or at champagne brunches on the White House lawn.

I would propose some legislation that would make the world a better place, sit in on important committees, and do all the stuff that lawmakers do to represent their constituencies well while also working on behalf of a grateful nation. People would beg me to run for president, but I would always divert those rumors and requests, saying that I had no ambition for such a job and that I was just happy to be serving where I was.

Things were going to be great.

I thought for sure this dream would come true. And even the ultimate guide to future success, the high school yearbook, agreed with me, practically solidifying my dream as a quite certain possibility. In the section detailing what each member of the class of 2001 of Pryor High School would be doing in ten years, this is what was listed beside my name:

Oklahoma State Senator (with a smoking hot wife).

Okay, maybe I added that last part, but the point is, my dream was even being realized by my peers at one point.

This dream was going to come true. I just knew it. Everything was lining up perfectly.

But things changed.

As some people like to say, "Life happened."

But what does that even mean, "life happened"? Does that mean no one gets to live out their dreams? After all, "life happens" to everyone. Is it something we're just supposed to accept as the natural order of things? I don't think so. The truth is, I made choices that had consequences. Those consequences – good, bad, or indifferent – altered who I was for a time and pushed me further and further away from my dream.

Life didn't "happen." *Lance* happened.

What about you? When you were younger and dared to dream about your future, what did it look like? Did it resemble anything like the life you're living today? For many of us the answer is no. We're not living the dreams of our natural, pure youth. Somewhere along the way our paths have been altered. For some of you, the road took a sharp turn one night when you were least expecting it; for others your journey resembles a slow progressive tilt that, over the years, has you headed east when you initially planned to go west.

Maybe you're one of the few who is living out the dreams of your youth, but you're beginning to realize that dream wasn't yours at all, but your parents'. It sure seems from the outside like life is good and that you are humming right along, but inside you feel that, though God has something great for you, you just don't know if your life could stand a new, different dream.

What if you were to close your eyes right now and envision your dream life ten years down the road? Go ahead, do it. Really let yourself go wild here: what would it look like? Who would be in your life? Are you married to that perfect spouse? What would you be doing with your life? With your occupation? Are you a counselor? A teacher? An author? A CEO? Are you running your own business, one you created from an idea sparked inside your head? Where would you live? Off in the mountains? On the East Coast? Near the water? Or would you just stay right where you are? In the same town? Same state or country?

Would you be pursuing your lifelong dream, the one you've dreamt about since you were young? Or would you have let it go in favor of something else, like a bigger dream or a lifestyle you would never have imagined for yourself in a million years?

What does *your* dream look like? Does it have a feel? Does it have a particular smell, like crisp ocean air or the earthy plains? Is it as ordinary as monetary success or as audacious as a game-changing invention or mission? This is *your* dream. What will it look like? There are no limitations; this is your do-over dream. There is no one here to stop you. Nothing in your way. You are the conductor, you are the pilot – so where are you going?

All these things were in my mind when I was younger, when my life was an unexplored road that stretched for miles before me. I had my next ten years all planned out. Yep, I knew where I was going and let me tell you, it was going to be awesome! It was kind of like that Dr. Seuss book, *Oh, The Places You'll Go!* You know, the one your mom gives you the night of your high school graduation (at least that's what *my* mom did). I read it and cried. A lot. I tend to do that. Cry, not read. Anyway, instead of the places we'd go, when I was growing up, my mental book could've been titled, *Oh, The Dreams I Have!* I was big dreamer. I still am. And like I said, as I was about to leave high school to go take on the world I had some incredible dreams.

Oh, what a nightmare it became.

Instead of my dreams of family, money, power, bright smiles, and a career in politics, here's what I got: divorce, depression, addiction, and despair.

An unexpected child, a hurried marriage, a prison of insecurities, unresolved resentments, paralyzing fear, and ten long years of chemical dependency that took away my dream, my marriage and, for a time, my precious children.

How did it happen? It happened because of choices I made, actions I took, and reactions I had based on false evidence and my own immature self-counsel. In short, I screwed it up. I thought I was invincible. Bulletproof. Indestructible.

I was wrong.

Life can get away from us very easily, and the dreams of our youth can fall away due to the choices we make – whether we made those choices mistakenly or whether they were forced upon us by the circumstances surrounding us (being mindful that sometimes we find ourselves in uncontrollable negative circumstances through no fault of our own, while other times our poor choices are the things that put us in negative circumstances).

No matter what dreams we have or what choices we make, we all learn this inevitable truth about life eventually: there is pain involved.

Pain is the common denominator that ties us all together.

So then the question becomes… what will we do with the pain?

I know what *I* did, and it wasn't pretty.

CHAPTER 2

HERE COMES THE PAIN

In April of 1755, after nine years of scholarly toil, writer, poet, and lexicographer Samuel Johnson published a groundbreaking work of literature. This marvelous volume was so intense that it was about a foot and a half tall, and when opened would span almost two feet. It became Johnson's most famous work, and, over the next 150 years, also became highly influential on other works of its type.

It was a dictionary.

The dictionary, actually. Formally titled *A Dictionary of the English Language*, Johnson's masterwork was the first of its kind. There had been a few attempts at dictionaries that codified English before Johnson's, but his was the first to take an all-encompassing look not just at the English language, but also at how people used it. Johnson didn't want to prescribe how words *should* be used; rather, he was more interested in looking at describing how they *were actually* used, both in common conversation and throughout English literature that had been generated up to that point in history.

Johnson not only wrote definitions for words but also came up with descriptions of how they were used and set forth explanations on how they were put together to create communication. Johnson's dictionary was also the first to illustrate word usage through quotations from literature. Want to know how to use, say, *yonder* in a sentence? Johnson had your back with a quote from *Romeo and Juliet*: "But, soft! What light through *yonder* window breaks?"

Johnson's dictionary was a runaway success, despite its enormous cost (it would be just over $500 in today's currency). People wanted it because they wanted to (literally) be on the same page when it came to the meanings of words individually and language in general.

They wanted definition.

While Johnson's achievement was a marvelous contribution to English language, in some ways it has created a now-pervasive mindset that exists among us. Because when we get into a disagreement about the way a word should be used in conversation, or whether it's even a *word* at all, where do we turn? To the dictionary, right?

We love the idea of an external authority to tell us how things are defined. If that's what the book says, then that's how it is, right? This can be wonderful and helpful, up to a certain point.

Until we start letting our failures define us.

Because our failures and our flaws are writing a dictionary full of lies about us, and if we consult that dictionary as the authority on who we are – if we allow that dictionary to define us – then we're going to start believing a bunch of stuff that is flat-out untrue.

Look, we all have failures, and we all have flaws. That's one of the givens of just being alive. There's not a perfect person among us, and the sooner we can accept that about ourselves, the better. But it's tempting to begin to magnify the faults and failures in our lives and minimize the good stuff, and when we do that, we're consulting the wrong dictionary.

That's what happened to me. I started believing the lie that my failures and flaws made me a loser. And once I started believing that lie, it began to compound in my mind until I felt buried under a landslide of self-doubt and insecurity. *I've messed up too much*, I would think. *There's no going back now. I'm a failure, I'm a fraud. My dreams are dead.*

That led to an even greater spiral, which led to my divorce, which only reconfirmed all the negative stuff I believed about myself that my flawed dictionary was defining for me. It told me all the naysayers in the world were right, and that I wasn't going to go anywhere in life.

If we let it, this is the dictionary that our pain will write for us.

If we let it, pain will steal our joy and derail our dreams.

You may have already experienced something like this. How has pain stolen your joy? What parts of your life have been stung by pain? How did you react to them? Did you open up the dictionary that pain wrote and start believing the definitions you found there? Did you let pain push you further and deeper into a hole you dug for yourself?

This very thing happened to one of my friends. Let's call him Jason. Jason grew up in a fairly typical suburban neighborhood, in one of those nondescript houses you can find along just about any street in northeast Oklahoma. Driving by, you would have no reason to think anything strange or different would be going on inside Jason's house, nothing illegal or shameful.

But that was far from the case.

Because ever since Jason was a small child, he had to live with a distorted reality; his adult neighbor would periodically come over and sexually abuse him. A pain that no child should ever feel was repeatedly forced upon Jason and, as a result, he felt unworthy and unaccepted. The actions of this evil adult created a series of lies that told Jason he was different. That he was weird. That he needed to keep all those feelings to himself.

So that's what Jason did. Over the years as he grew up and the abuse finally stopped, Jason internalized his pain and all those lies, pushing himself farther and farther from who he really was. Instead of feeling normal, instead of developing the sense of self-worth that is crucial to our survival in adulthood, Jason instead developed a warped perception of himself as a stranger. He hated who he was, and so he sought an escape from himself and from the constant negative feelings he had toward himself.

This self-hatred pushed him into experimenting with drugs and alcohol. All he wanted was something to numb his pain for a little bit, to get away from the lies that blared in his mind without stopping. His experimentation turned into an addiction, which gave him what he needed to get out from under the weight of that pain, even if only for a brief moment.

But, as every addict finds out eventually, addiction only drives us further from our natural selves, laying a blanket of self-deception on top of our pain and doing nothing to actually deal with it. Instead, we hope the cover-up will be enough, only to find that the cover slips off eventually and sends us back to that raw, vulnerable place where we don't know how to deal with the feelings and pain of our past.

Jason tried to cover up his shame with a blanket of heroin. He tried, unsuccessfully, to kill those lies and silence those voices. Death by injection.

But slowly, year after year, he was only killing himself.

Jason was finally able to find a breakthrough; he sought treatment and found the strength to expose his secret and tell someone about the horrors he'd endured as a child.

By exposing the pain of his past, Jason was able to finally address it. He was able to shine a light on those memories and see the lies for what they were, and finally, at long last, learn that what happened to him *wasn't his fault.* Someone had caused him pain, someone had dealt him a blow he couldn't control, and now he was able to acknowledge that. By looking at that pain and at his own vulnerability, Jason was able to begin to move toward the light and convert his pain into a motivational force that pulled him into sobriety. Through hard work and no small amount of difficulty, Jason is living free today.

Or maybe you'll relate to my buddy Matthew, who made a terrible mistake one night that changed his life irrevocably. Matthew was out partying one night, had a little too much to drink, and then decided to drive himself home. Needless to say, Matthew's alcoholic impairment got in the way of his critical thinking; he was involved in a traffic collision that took another person's life. Vehicular manslaughter.

The memories of that fateful decision and the horrors of that night stayed with Matthew long after the following morning, casting a long shadow that darkened his future for many years beyond the one that he spent in prison. The results of Matthew's actions led to a never-ending monologue in his mind: *You're reckless. You should've been the one who died. You don't deserve to be alive. You don't deserve to be free. You got off easy. You should be locked up for life. You took a life; you should lose yours.*

Matthew tried to drown those voices in alcohol, or at least shut them up with the drugs he forced through his body. He did all he could to medicate his shame into submission, spending years as an addict and bouncing in and out of treatment centers in a desperate attempt to find himself underneath all those layers of shame.

He still has trouble. Matthew still, as I write this, deals with the pain of that singular, devastating choice. He has punished himself because of his past pain, refusing to let himself off the hook for that accident. His pain has driven him to do things to himself and to those around him that only cause more hurt. But he's working through it now, and he's learning how to find peace in the midst of his pain.

And then there's me.

I was not the most well-behaved child, which often made things unnecessarily difficult for my father, a respected pastor in small-town Oklahoma. Any time I rebelled against our town's societal and cultural norms or got even a little out of line, my dad had to hear about it from just about everyone in his church, which meant I heard about it at home. But rather than using these negative outcomes as motivation to "straighten up and fly right," I continued making choices that pushed against the restrictions placed on me.

Certainly, I was growing up in a flawed culture that placed more emphasis on how things looked to the rest of the world than on what sort of damage they might have done to me. Right or wrong, that was the culture and environment in which I grew up, making it the culture and environment that influenced my choices. And my choices then influenced my parents' reactions to me, which were in turn informed by their own experiences, the culture and environment they'd each grown up in during their childhoods, and the one which they'd created together in adulthood. That all makes sense, right? Of course it does.

Anyway, this was the world I inhabited when my breaking point came. This was my world when I was eighteen years old and a senior in high school with a steady girlfriend.

And we found out we were pregnant.

After we came to grips with this ourselves, we knew it was time to tell our parents. Which meant it was time to tell *my* parents. I already knew it wasn't going to go well, but I had no idea ahead of time just how poorly it was going to pan out.

We sat down in the living room at my house – me, my girlfriend, my mother, and my father – and after a few tense

moments, I blurted out the sentence that had been thousands
of choices in the making and that would become the hinge
upon which my life would swing for the next ten years.

"Mom, Dad," I said, "we're pregnant."

I guess I'd been hoping against hope that there would
be a measure of grace and compassion for a couple of scared,
insecure teenagers who'd taken a sudden plunge into an
unconsidered adulthood. That's what I'd been hoping for. What
I got, however, was exactly what I expected.

My father sat there in disbelief, still and unmoving,
but I could tell by the look in his eyes that he was furious. My
mother, on the other hand, had no problem expressing her
anger and disappointment.

"How could you do this?" she said. "What will this do to
us? What are people going to think? Your father has worked so
hard to build a reputation as a godly man, and now *this*?"

It went on like that for awhile.

Before I continue this story, let me just say this right
now: my parents are good people. No, scratch that. They
are great people. The absolute best people, parents, and
grandparents a person could ever ask for. They were then and
they still are now, and I wouldn't be where I am today without

their generous, sacrificial help. My dad is the sole reason this book is even possible and my mother loves me so much that she's the one who practically kept me alive while I was in rehab.

I don't envy my mother and father the situation they were in with my troubled teenage self. I was a rebellious mess, and this was just the latest in a long line of screw-ups for me. But now that I *am* a parent, let me let you in on a secret about all parents: we don't know what we're doing. If you're a parent, you may be figuring this out even now, but it's true. Every parent in this world has an *idea* on how to go about raising kids, but even then they're just making stuff up as they go along, doing the best they can with what they have.

And that's what my folks were doing. Like it or not, they had a lot of pressure as pastors in a small town to maintain a certain outward image of piety and peace, and I'm sure that pressure weighed on them intensely. I'm sure there were also other internal parental pressures that erupted when my girlfriend and I sat in that living room and dropped a bomb on them, worries about taking care of me and their new grandchild, worries that were a complicated mixture of questions about resources, love, money, time, image, and a whole lot of other things.

I do not – for a single second – begrudge my parents for reacting the way they did. I understand it, today. I still wish they hadn't reacted that way, because, as you'll see, their reaction influenced some really, really negative and stupid decisions on my part. But while I can wish for a different outcome to a past event, I know I can't get it, and so instead I do what I *can do*, which is make peace with what happened and look forward to the future.

That's the power of hope.

Now that we've established this power, let's go back to that couch in my parents' living room and take a look at the fallout from the baby-shaped nuclear warhead my girlfriend and I had just dropped in there.

The first thing my parents did was ask my girlfriend to leave the house. She went outside, got in her car, and drove herself home. Alone. And I'm sure that was very much a reinforcement of her own feelings – that she was now alone in this world, a castaway, one of the few things our society often treats like it's radioactive: an unwed mother.

Now that the mother of my future child was out of the house, my parents were free to berate me and rake me over the coals, which they proceeded to do for the next hour, writing a symphony of parental disappointment built around the very basic theme of *How could you do this?* I was expected to sit and listen to it until they were finished, I suppose, but after an hour or so, I couldn't take anymore.

Every word they spoke, every dramatic gesture they made with their hands, every disgusted step they took as they paced around the room… it all told me very believable falsehoods about myself: that I was inferior. That I couldn't do anything right. That I was a failure and that I would always be a failure.

These are lies, of course. These thoughts are the opposite of hope, but in that moment, listening to my parents as they talked about me, about their reputation, about the judgment of the people within church they were pastoring, I believed it all. And the more I believed it, the more inevitable my defeat as a person seemed. I felt that if I didn't get my act together in the eyes of my parents, I was going to be rejected and abandoned, and that made me feel all the more terrible. Disappointments and fears were piling up on my heart, until it all got too heavy for me to hold.

So I ran.

I *literally ran.*

I bolted out of my parents' house and hoofed it across town to my girlfriend's house. I just wanted to be with someone who accepted me. I wanted to run away from the pain and toward something that could make me feel better – my relationship, alcohol, drugs, or sex – regardless of whether that thing was good for me or not.

I ran that night, my choices fueled by a bunch of lies pressed upon me by those small-town norms. I ran and I really didn't stop running for another ten years, until Jesus finally blocked my path with his arms outstretched, inviting my exhausted self to collapse in his embrace.

Looking back with the clarity provided by sobriety, experience, and history, I can see now that the main thing I'd been dealing with was pain. Pain was the invisible force that helped me to believe a bunch of lies and that spurred me out the front door that night.

A few clarifications about what I mean when I use the word *pain*. Sure, there's such a thing as physical pain, but there's also emotional pain. The pain of disappointment. The pain of rejection. The pain of abandonment and isolation. The pain of dejection. How you hurt as human being. The aches of life, the agony of loss, the embarrassment of ridicule, the loneliness of rejection, the debilitating doubt of insecurity, the stings of sadness, the discomfort of depression, the terror of a trauma, the madness of molestation, the wounds that break the surface of our heart.

This is the type of pain I'm talking about.

Sudden loss of life, a break up, a divorce, an embarrassing moment, a time when you were touched inappropriately, a time when you were forced to do something you didn't want to do, a fight, an accident, a lie, a secret, mistrust, public embarrassment, fraud, cheating, a broken heart.

When I say *pain*, I mean anything that negatively changes the way we feel about ourselves.

So have you experienced a painful moment like one I just described? Maybe what happened to you is not listed, but when I listed the others, the pain you experienced instantly came to mind. While we often know the pain is there, we can also often miss out on the realization of what it's doing to us. Pain is an insidious, creeping force that will take an immense toll on us if we let it.

Until that night, my pain was a nest of termites eating away at me from the inside out. Have you ever seen a tree that

fell because it was ridden with termites? It's an amazing sight.
This tree that was standing tall and proud for so many years
had been, unbeknownst to you, slowly and under the surface,
decimated. Its structure was being removed, little by little;
its core strength was being weakened. The casual observer at
ground level wouldn't be able to tell. But then, along comes
a storm or a powerful wind, and that's enough to topple the
whole tree.

That's what pain did to me.

That might be what it's doing to you.

Pain: Why and How It Happens

Thanks to the Fall, sin is everywhere. Blame it on Adam.
Blame it on the rain. Blame it on the gin, blame it on the
Henny… (Sorry, I got a little carried away there.) Regardless
of where the blame falls, we all struggle with sin, which you'll
see as I provide several examples throughout this book. Pain is
everywhere, because sin is everywhere.

But take heart: hope is everywhere as well.

The Apostle Paul speaks to this in the book of 2
Corinthians. He spends part of Chapter 11 running down all
the ways he's suffered for the gospel, including shipwrecks,

imprisonments, beatings, and days without food, water, or sleep. He calls these "boasts," and then writes, in verse 30, "If I must boast, I will boast of the things that show my weakness."

Next, Paul talks about how even this type of boasting could make him conceited. And so what has God done in response to this? Let's pick it up halfway through verse 7 of Chapter 12: "Therefore, in order to keep me from becoming conceited, I was given a thorn in my flesh, a messenger of Satan, to torment me. Three times I pleaded with the Lord to take it away from me. But he said to me, 'My grace is sufficient for you, for my power is made perfect in weakness.' Therefore I will boast all the more gladly about my weaknesses, so that Christ's power may rest on me. That is why, for Christ's sake, I delight in weaknesses, in insults, in hardships, in persecutions, in difficulties. For when I am weak, then I am strong."

I love that last line! I mean, I love the whole passage, but that final sentence especially is such a hope-bringer for me. Even a guy as obviously blessed by God as the Apostle Paul, someone who was in constant communion with the Almighty and who wrote a significant portion of a sacred text – *even that guy* dealt with pain.

As a Christian, I am convinced that while there is a

God who loves and cares for us, unfortunately there is also an enemy who equally hates us. He practices in pain. It's his chief weapon. And he's always crafting a way to bring it upon us. He *likes* to bring the pain. People aren't our main issue as much as the emotional and psychological pain and torment the enemy is always trying to drum up and use against us.

Now, a word about Paul and that "thorn in the flesh," a "messenger of Satan" which was "given" to him in order to "torment" him. There has been a great theological debate throughout the centuries of Christianity as to what exactly this "thorn" was. There are many theories, from a debilitating illness to a tormented mind to whatever medical ailment has been in the news a lot lately.

It doesn't matter. What matters is how Paul thought about it, how he dealt with it, and how he lived his life in spite of it. Maybe you're experiencing a pain that was brought on you by someone else; physical pain in the form of violence or emotional pain from enduring something like your parents' divorce. I don't believe God did those things *to* you in order to keep you from growing conceited. In fact, I believe God hates that bad things have happened to you and caused you pain.

But I also believe God can redeem you in the midst of it

and turn your pain into a platform. How? We know that pain is here on earth, and while there's not much we can do about its presence, there is *a lot* we can do about its power. To do that, we must revisit it.

I know it isn't easy to travel back in your memory to the time when pain first struck. But for a brief moment, if you can, I want you to go back there one more time and think about the way it made you feel.

As I wrote about a few of my painful moments for this book – including the moments you just read about – I forced myself to relive them once more and to do the best I could to pinpoint what I was *actually feeling* in those moments. So what did I pick up on as I tried that out? Mainly, I noticed feelings of rejection and doubt. And for years those were the two primary fears I lived with on a daily basis. Basically, in the back of my mind, I carried around an overwhelming fear that people would reject me, and because of that feeling, I began to tell myself I was never good enough, which caused me to act and react in ways that fulfilled my very feelings – making them come true all too often and creating even more pain.

Those fears became like leeches all over my body that sucked the life right out of me. I lost the confidence I had grown up with. I lost the connection to God I had so enjoyed at times during my life. I lost what it meant to be me.

Over the years, the weight of my fears dragged me down, changed me, altered everything about me.

It changed the way I worked. It changed the way I parented. It changed my marriage. It changed my relationships with friends. It changed the way I viewed God – and ultimately it changed my perspective on how God viewed me.

Rejection and doubt eventually led me to have such low self-worth that I didn't care what I did to myself. I had no honor, no character, and no morals. And that's when I started medicating myself to escape the reality of what I was becoming.

The downfall and destruction of my life are a great example of the way the enemy loves to work. He pulls a moment from your life when you were hurt and keeps it right in front of your face by lying to you. Telling you that what happened to you was your fault. That something's wrong with you that caused this to happen until you pick up fears associated with that experience.

Pain is a hunter that often comes camouflaged, sneaking up on us all dark and hidden inside a blind. We don't notice it, because it doesn't wear one of those garish orange hats, but also because it's like the progressive disease of addiction. It starts out small and seemingly insignificant, then builds and builds and builds until it overtakes our lives without us realizing it's even happened, much less knowing how to get out of it.

Pain comes from the choices we make that we carry with us, as well as the choices others have made on our behalf that irrevocably scar us. Look, I know we live in a society that celebrates individualism and personal responsibility, but the fact remains that, while we are indeed a product of our choices and are responsible for the actions we take and the reactions we make, other people influence us, too.

When an adult abuses a child, that will influence them.

When a boss lays off an employee, removing their sole source of income, that will influence them.

When a child takes their own life, that will influence their friends and family.

When a person is born into poverty, that will influence them.

When a drunk driver takes away someone you love, that will influence you.

When your spouse cheats, that will influence you.

When your parents say hurtful things, that will

influence you.

This list of pain-filled influences could go on and on. We can't escape painful situations, and we can't escape other people's reactions to those situations, either. We can only do the best we can to make good choices in the midst of the pain that comes our way.

Because the pain is coming.

But that's okay, because so is the hope.

CHAPTER 3

FEAR DRIVES MORE THAN YOU THINK

"I cost our team the game."

– Chris Webber

I'm a huge basketball fan. I love to play it and I love to watch it, and as a result I've noticed something about that sport specifically that also applies to all sports in general. Namely, this:

It's amazing how many game decisions are based on fear.

If you follow sports at all, or even if you don't, you'll notice that those athletes who wind up being great are often referred to as "fearless." They're the one who want the ball in the clutch – the great quarterbacks who take risks in order to deliver the perfectly thrown pass or the timeless basketball superstar who always wants to be the one to take the last shot. These are the ones who don't get rattled when the championship is on the line, the ones who don't play afraid.

The reason they're so great is because they're so rare; but and even some of the greatest and most historic players can sometimes slip into playing from a place of fear. Take, for example, Chris Webber, one of the most celebrated college basketball players of all time, and the heart of the famous "Fab Five Freshman" who played for the University of Michigan Wolverines in the early 1990s.

Webber, along with Juwan Howard, Jalen Rose, Jimmy King, and Ray Jackson, took the college basketball world by storm when they burst onto the scene with their long, baggy shorts and hip-hop swagger. They weren't just freshmen; they were flat-out fresh, playing team-oriented ball that was fun to watch – and successful. They started knocking down opponents left and right and made it all the way to the championship game of the NCAA tournament before losing to Duke University by a mammoth twenty points.

The next year, expectations were high for the team – after all, they'd reached the finals as freshmen (unheard of at the time) and lost to one of the greatest college basketball programs of all time. Nothing to hang your head about there. But now that Michigan's "Fab Five" were no longer freshmen but were indeed on the map, it was time to show the world what they were made of.

They had another dream season, another bull-in-a-china-shop run through the NCAA tournament, and another championship appearance, and this time, they were in the game the whole way. Facing off against the University of North Carolina, Michigan was competitive for 39 minutes and 49 seconds until, at the end, Chris Webber played afraid.

Here's what happened. The Wolverines were down by two points with eleven seconds to play, which is an eternity in college basketball. You have eleven seconds to score at least two points to tie it up or three points to win, and you have the celebrated "Fab Five" on the floor? Those are odds most fan bases would've take in just about any instance.

The Wolverines inbounded the ball and Webber took it across half-court where he was immediately double-teamed by two players from North Carolina. Suddenly panicking, Webber signaled for a timeout to reset the offense for what would be the game-winning play.

Except there was one slight problem.

Michigan was out of timeouts.

And you aren't allowed to call for timeout when you don't have any timeouts left.

Instead of having the ball on their side of the floor to set up the winning bucket, Michigan was assessed a technical foul and North Carolina got the ball back. All that was left of the game were some desperate fouls, some North Carolina free throws, and that was it. The North Carolina Tar Heels were crowned champs and the Michigan Wolverines went back to Ann Arbor as runners-up once more.

Because of a little fear.

Once you start to notice how much of a role fear plays in sports, you start to see it everywhere. Coaches, players, even officials – many of them play it safe instead of going all out. When football team is down by seven points with a few minutes remaining in the game and is facing a fourth and two, more often than not the coach will radio in a punt or a kick instead of going for the first down. Or a great hitter in baseball is at the plate with his team down by a run in the ninth inning. He gets afraid of striking out and so he watches a perfectly hittable ball rocket past him with the bat still on his shoulder, striking out anyway.

These are the routine moments of sports. It's why the opposite – a touchdown on fourth and twenty-seven or a walk-off home run – makes the highlight reels on ESPN. We get so used to being driven by fear that it has become the default expectation; when someone plays fearlessly, they get toasted on TV and lauded online.

So what's the root of this? Where does it come from? None of the elite athletes we see on television or read about online or in magazines started out as elite. More than likely, they've spent multiple years developing their craft, honing it, working on it in practice sessions and in games. From childhood into adulthood, they've grown into themselves and into their understanding of the game they play.

And chances are good that they've taken more than a few risks during that time, and that when they did, the risk didn't always work out. So then what happened? They got yelled at by some coach on the sideline for that mistake, and they got the message loud and clear: Don't screw up.

When you approach the game with that mentality – just

be safe, don't screw up, protect the lead – you are giving way to fear. You are allowing the mistakes of your past to cloud your judgment in the present, which will ultimately affect your future.

When you look beneath the surface, you'll find that fear is a driving force behind many of the decisions we make. We stumble into some pain in life and that creates a fear. We're afraid we'll be hurt again, so we modify our decisions based on that. If it's a repeated hurt, then we make determinations to escape it or remove it through some means (retributive violence, calling the cops, relocation, quitting a job, you name it – we are very creative in the ways we try to escape fear).

Even when we make hopeful choices to live a better life or to take a risk and seize an opportunity (or try to create our own opportunities), often those decisions are a reaction to fear! Think about it. How many people do you know who have made some life-altering positive decision because they were afraid of what would happen if they didn't? Someone who started their own business because they don't want to work for someone else for the rest of their lives is motivated partly because they're afraid of what they perceive as a dull life of repetitive toil.

I learned about this fear-based reaction to life through

a program I went through in the early part of my recovery. One of the many things that rehabilitating yourself teaches is how to really examine your life and determine *why* you do the things you do.

Part of this program involved me walking through my early history – starting from childhood, through the time period in which I started using and then beyond – to identify what sorts of pain I'd endured… and then to identify what fears were created as a result of that pain. The idea was that we all base some of our fears, whether we realize it or not, on the types of pain we've had to deal with. This program was all about recognizing the fear and examining how it had skewed our relationships, our confidence, our self-image, our theology, you name it.

Looking back through that lens, I can see that I was afraid. I was afraid of myself, afraid of my failures, afraid of who I was. I had a deep-rooted fear that I couldn't operate without drugs and booze, that I wasn't enough on my own. I was still believing the lies that had come along with the pain of being rejected by my parents – and really the society that they represented – in our living room that day I told them I was going to be a father.

They had unknowingly, through their reactions, communicated to me that I was a failure and not worth loving. They were completely unaware that they had taught me I was unconfident. They didn't know they'd ripped aside whatever thin veneer I'd painted onto my own hollow sense of self and shown me how poorly I felt about myself.

But that's where I was. I was in pain, I felt horrible, and I needed something to make me feel better and instill some sense of confidence, regardless of how inauthentic that confidence was or how damaging its methods and outcomes.

So I gave in to the fear and immersed myself in drugs, which in turn gave me the ability to maneuver past the pain and fear and to put up a loud, brash front that projected confidence. But like the fearful wizard in Oz, it really was all just an illusion.

Fear tempts us throughout life – whether we fear the past, the future, a familiar hurt/wound/injury, missed opportunities, or something else altogether..

Fear wants to convince you it's bigger than it really is so that you'll buy into its lies and carry it around with you. How so? Try this example. Every Sunday night at 10:00 I go to my AA home group meeting. I've been going for a while now and I really enjoy both ending my weekend and starting my week with a bunch of people who are crazy like I am. It makes me feel normal.

One night, one of those crazy folks gave me one of the best analogies I've ever heard when it comes to carrying around the pains, fears, and decisions of our past. The chairperson explained it like this: "Picture fear like a backpack. The first time you make a major mistake or someone does something major to you, you put on that backpack. Then for the next twenty years every time something reminds you of that moment, you put a rock in that backpack. Pretty soon you can't take that backpack off, it's become a part of you, and it affects everything you do."

Man, that guy was right on! It made perfect sense when I heard it. Not because I thought other people do that, but because *I know* I did that. A lot. I strapped that backpack on when I ran out of my house at eighteen years old and had been chucking rocks into it every day since then, letting the pain of my past direct the course of my future.

I don't know about you, but I'm tired of living with those burdens on my shoulders. I don't want to carry around feelings of fear, rejection, and doubt. I want to live confidently and true to the person I was created to be. And that's not always a pretty picture, but I want to be okay with that. I want to be comfortable in my own skin.

Do you?

I'm guessing you struggle with at least *some* of the same fears that I struggle do. At least I hope so; otherwise I'm the only crazy one.

As I've gotten more and more outspoken about my past, sharing my story in more and more places, I've had a slew of opportunities to speak intimately with people who are struggling. From Facebook Messenger, e-mail, and texting to sit-down lunches, Google Hangouts, and regular ol' phone calls, you name it and I've done it. It's wild – the moment you begin to express your pain, people instantly want to express theirs. We'll go more in-depth on this later, but what this has taught me is that no one is immune to pain. We all have been through it, and because of the pain of the past, we all are living with fears driving and directing our lives, sending us down paths we never intended to travel, getting us off the course of God's intended will for our lives and distancing us from our dreams.

From where you're sitting, it may feel like certain trials only happen to people like you. Maybe you're a single parent, facing the fear of guilt every day because of a difficult decision you had to make, a decision that forever changed your life. You've probably had moments where you think there's no way those perfect-looking families – with the husband with the steady, high-paying job at the oil company and the wife who blogs about decorating her perfect little house and their two sweater-vested, grinning kids – ever feel what you're feeling. Well let me tell you, I've met with lots of those special little families and I'll let you in on a secret: they feel just as jacked-up as you sometimes do. Guilt doesn't discriminate

Maybe you're a pastor facing the fear of inadequacy. You've probably thought to yourself a time or two that there's no way another pastor feels as insignificant and ill-equipped as you do. You've said to yourself, *All I see are these mega-church pastors with their skinny jeans,* Duck Dynasty-*wannabe beards, and the seventeen new campuses they're launching this year. I can't do that! I don't even own any skinny jeans. I only own fat guy jeans and rock a mustache that makes Rollie Fingers look like Higgins from "Magnum P.I."* Well, let me tell you something: first off, mustaches are cool, so don't worry about that. Secondly, I meet with pastors all the time from churches like that, and they are just as freaked out and filled with doubt as you are. Insecurity doesn't discriminate.

You might be like me and some of my friends. You may have made a *lot* of bad choices in your past and are struggling with fear of the future. You're probably somewhere between 25-40, and everywhere you look you see guys and gals your age getting new jobs, scaling the corporate ladder (I've never seen a ladder at a corporate office, by the way), getting married to someone whose looks would be filed under Suburban Hotness, buying their first house, going on vacations. But when you look at yourself, all you can see is a future filled with counseling sessions and date nights with Dave Ramsey. And this fear of the future is weighing you down because you think there's no way these people are afraid of whether the next paycheck is coming or if they'll ever find the perfect job. Well, let me tell you something: I meet with tons of single folks, myself included (in fact, I'm my biggest client), and let me reassure you, many of them are scared of their future. In fact, they are terrified – and the ones running around being extravagant are the most fearful of all. Fear of the future does not discriminate.

Or maybe you're like the dozens of parents I work with who are battling the fear of the unknown on a nightly basis. Your son or daughter is wrapped in the grip of addiction and you sit at home pleading with God every day to bring them home – and to bring them home *safely*. You've probably thought hundreds of times that no one is enduring the agony of this uncertainty like you are. You feel helpless and hurt, and worst of all you don't know what to do. All you can see is happiness and joy in the families in your neighbor or at your church and you think, *No one else lives with this fear like I do.* Well, let me compassionately and warmly tell you: you are not alone. While it may not be the news you really want to hear, let it be a comfort to you to know that what you are facing you do not have to face alone. You can accept that this pain is bringing you down and take the courageous step to find some support and help. Because fear of the unknown doesn't discriminate.

Again: no one is immune to pain and fear – or the craziness that can come along with them. Crazy lives in every closet, whether it's a walk-in or not. No one escapes life without being deeply impacted by pain. There is shame in everyone's shadow; the relief comes when we bring it into the light.

Fear is actually an age-old problem, going all the way back to the story of Adam, Eve, the garden of Eden, and a smooth-talking serpent. You probably know the story: in the book of Genesis, God creates the world, plunks a beautiful garden down in the middle of it, and then creates Adam and

Eve to take care of it. He tells them they can eat from any tree except one, which is the Tree of the Knowledge of Good and Evil. And that's where we see the serpent (traditionally understood to be a manifestation of the devil – it was, after all, a *talking snake*) use the lie of fear to motivate Adam and Eve into some stupid decisions.

In Genesis 3, we read all about the serpent's techniques and tactics. I imagine the him sidling up to Eve like a creepy, trenchcoat-wearing guy at a party, slipping his arm around her, and using an innocent question to play on her fears. What does he ask? "Did God really say, 'You must not eat from any tree in the garden?'"

Eve responds with confidence, but I think her response also masks a little bit of fear. She tries a little *too* hard to make her point: "We may eat fruit from the trees in the garden, but God did say, 'You must not eat fruit from the tree that is in the middle of the garden, and you must not touch it, or you will die.'" If you check out the original command given a chapter earlier, you'll notice God didn't say anything either way about touching the fruit.

And so what does the serpent say? Seeing his opening, he slips in a subtle fear: "'You will not certainly die,' the serpent said to the woman. 'For God knows that when you eat from it your eyes will be opened, and you will be like God, knowing good and evil.'"

Did you see the fear? It's subtle, but it's there.

It's the fear of missing out.

The serpent is telling Eve: *Are you sure about that? You can be like God! You can know the difference between good and evil – think about what you could do with that kind of information! Think of how great your life could be!*

Don't miss this opportunity!

Act now! Operators are standing by!

And so what happens? Eve buys the lie, gives into her fear, convincing herself it's really because she wants to get some wisdom, and plucks some fruit off the tree to eat it. She doesn't want to miss this opportunity to be like God! So off comes the fruit, in go her teeth, chomp chomp. Nom-nom. Mmm, this is pretty good. Adam, you want some of this? Here you go, dude.

Yes, according to the story we read in Genesis 3:6, Adam was standing right there the whole time, and he had no problem digging in to the forbidden fruit, just like Eve had. Once they do that, their "eyes… were opened" and the realization hit them that they were naked, which brought a quick helping of shame, which led them to the decision to sew together some fig leaves to hide their nakedness.

All of these actions came about because of fear. They took the fruit because they were afraid to miss out. Then they were ashamed because they were afraid of themselves. Then they covered themselves up because they were afraid of their nakedness.

But covering themselves wasn't enough, because now they know they've disobeyed God's commands and are afraid of the repercussions. So, in addition to covering over their nakedness, Adam and Eve cover their tracks and hide among the trees when they hear God walking toward them, prompting God to call out, "Where are you?"

Adam hears the question and reveals his motivation: "I heard you in the garden, and I was afraid because I was naked; so I hid."

He was afraid.

Fear escalates. Let it in, and the result of fear will always be to make you more afraid.

And here's the ironic thing: Adam and Eve were afraid of missing out and acted on that fear… which resulted in getting kicked out of the garden of Eden. The thing they were afraid would happen is *the very thing that happened to them.*

Even worse: they already lived in perfection – what on earth could they possibly miss out on? If you were put in a complete paradise, with all your needs met, with the perfect companion, and with regular time spent walking through this paradise with God Himself, would you do *anything* to mess that up? Yet it wasn't enough for Adam and Eve; their fear of missing out on something "better" led to their removal from the best thing they could ever possibly have.

Fear is such an unreliable motivator. God had already given Adam and Eve perfection. He'd given them everything they needed – including an identity – and they *still* had trouble buying into it.

So if you're giving yourself a hard time over the ways you've reacted to pain, or to the fear it's created within you, don't beat yourself up. If Adam and Eve, living in a sin-free paradise, couldn't tune out fear completely, then you sure won't be able to do it either.

But there *is* a lot you *can* do to combat the fear and to turn your pain into something beautiful. It all starts with believing what God says about you, who He says you *really* are, and how that differs from what you tend to think about yourself. And that's where we turn our attention next.

CHAPTER 4

FINDING YOU AGAIN

It's amazing to consider that we are, each of us, a God-created and eternal being with a tremendous power to affect change around the world… and that most of us don't walk in that identity. Why, that would be like being a folk singer who recorded a couple of albums in the 1970s, then faded into obscurity and a life as a blue-collar laborer, then getting a phone call thirty years later informing you that not only had your albums had gone multi-platinum in South Africa and Australia – making you hugely popular in both countries -- but that you had inadvertently and unknowingly contributed to the eradication of apartheid, South Africa's government-mandated racism.

But that could never happen, right?

Except, as you may have guessed given my oddly specific example, for the time it did.

The singer was a man named Sixto Rodriguez, who performed in and around Detroit, Michigan in the late 1960s and early 1970s under the name "Rodriguez." A couple of record producers still coasting on the success of the Motown era heard him in a dingy club one day, were impressed with his raw folk sound and his highly political lyrics, and brought him into their studio to make a record.

The album was called *Cold Fact*, and it was released in 1970 in the United States to little fanfare. Practically no one bought it. The same held true for Rodriguez's follow-up album, *Coming from Reality*, released in the United States the following year. With his music career going nowhere, Rodriguez essentially retired from the music business and instead stepped into a life of blue-collar labor.

As the story goes, at least as the documentary film *Searching for Sugar Man* tells it, of the few people who had purchased *Cold Fact*, one of them was an American woman who was then dating someone who lived in South Africa. She flew over to visit him and brought the album with her and wound up leaving it there. And like a virus of positivity introduced into a foreign population, the album found a welcome host and spread rapidly in popularity.

Inspired by Rodriguez's observations about the injustice often perpetrated by those in power, some of South Africa's major civil rights icons began to demonstrate against the systemic racist oppression found in the policy of apartheid. Rodriguez's music also lit a fire in other South African artists and musicians, who began to find inspiration for their own music, using their new songs as a means to turn the tide on the nation's horrific racial injustice.

The rest is history. More and more people fought against the policy, which led to international support to end apartheid, which, after a long fight, was finally officially done away with in 1994.

I'm not saying Rodriguez ended apartheid – I'm saying his music was one of the many, many things that inspired people to fight against it. It was so inspiring, in fact, that his album was released in South Africa in 1971 and wound up going platinum over there – which means it sold at least a million copies.

And Rodriguez had no idea.

He was a trailblazer and an unequivocal success as a musician and songwriter (however you wish to measure that "success;" I understand that is a nebulous term that has different meanings for different people), but he was completely unaware of that, instead scraping out a living with his hands in the decreasingly economically mobile Detroit. Instead of using his hands to make music, he was using them to paint houses or demolish them or whatever else needed to be done.

He was completely ignorant of the fact of who he really was. Who he could be.

You know who he reminds me of? A guy named Gideon. We read about Gideon in the book of Judges Chapter 6, where we first learn that the nation of Israel has been overrun by people called the Midianites, who were like a plague of locusts that oppressed the Israelites, destroying their crops and herds and making life miserable for them so they could possess the land.

By the time our man Gideon comes on the scene, this had been going on for seven years, and the Israelites were definitely bowed down under the weight of the Midianite oppression. Things were so bad that the first time in this story that we see Gideon, he's hiding out in a winepress he's using the

press to thresh wheat, terrified that the Midianites will find out
he's able to feed himself and his family.

While the Midianites don't uncover Gideon's subterfuge,
you know who *does* find him in that winepress? God (of
course that was going to be the answer). God gives Gideon the
lowdown, calling him a mighty warrior.

A mighty warrior!

Gideon pushes back on that idea and the Lord tells him
this, which we read in Judges 6:14: "Go in the strength you have
and save Israel out of Midian's hand. Am I not sending you?"

Go in the *strength you have*. You'll notice God didn't say
to Gideon, "Go in the strength I'll give you." Nor did He say,
"Go and hope I meet you there."

Go in the strength you have.

God was saying something about Gideon that Gideon
wasn't ready to believe. Gideon needed to see himself as God
already saw him, and so God starts off strong, calling him a
mighty warrior who already has strength. Pretty cool.

But it didn't stop there. Because Gideon was determined
to talk his way out of this assignment, he revealed how he
already thought about himself, which we read in the next verse:
"'Pardon me, my lord,' Gideon replied, 'but how can I save

Israel? My clan is the weakest in Manasseh, and I am the least in my family.'"

Gideon counters God's declarations about him with declarations of his own, basically saying, "I don't believe you, God, because all I know about me is that I'm weak and from a tiny clan that cannot possibly be the one to deliver Israel."

What a difference perspective can make.

What's remarkable, though, is how *persistent* God is toward Gideon. He just won't take no for an answer, and He even goes so far as to take supernaturally dramatic lengths to remind Gideon that he *is in fact a mighty warrior.*

Gideon finally believed it, by the way. After a few halting tests and trials, Gideon accepts the Godly perspective about himself and leads Israel to a mighty victory over the Israelites (for more on the exploits of Gideon, read Judges 6-7 [or watch *A Bug's Life*]).

The point is: if you can change your perspective and begin to see yourself as God sees you, it will change your life irrevocably.

Because of the pain of your past, you might feel like a sinful failure who is destined always to be fighting off your personal demons. But God sees you as a victorious warrior who can – and will – fight to the end.

Because of the pain of your past, you might feel like a slave to your sin. But God sees you as His own liberated child, free to live according to His pleasure.

Because of the pain of your past, you might feel like a worthless piece of flesh whose only value lies in using your body. But God sees you as a unique and wonderful creation who is worth so much more than casual, indifferent sex.

Because of the pain of your past, you might feel like nothing more than a walking pile of uncontrollable impulses. But God sees you as a person of self-control, capable of clamping down on the mental lies of the enemy.

Because of the pain of your past, you might feel like a boiling pot of rage, constantly on the verge of spilling over onto those you love. But God sees you as a bringer of peace and patience, forgiving others just as He has forgiven you.

The point is: you *simply are not* what the pain of your past says about you. That pain doesn't have to define you; God does. He says you're special. Unique. Set apart. Chosen. Accepted. Set free. No longer a slave to darkness but instead a child of the light.

You are not the sum of your mistakes, your poor

choices, and all the suffering you've endured at the hands of others. No, you're much, much more than that. You've been extended a hand of forgiveness and redemption! You have been made new!

One of my favorite passages in the Bible is found in 2 Corinthians 5:17. It reads: "Therefore, if anyone is in Christ, the new creation has come: The old has gone, the new is here!"

We can lose track of hope because we let it get buried underneath a bunch of old stuff that used to define us. It can covered over by layers and layers of lies, pain, hurt, and fear, until it is completely unrecognizable.

We have to learn to see it. To stand on our tiptoes and reach a higher level so we can try to see from God's perspective, because that higher perspective provides us with clarity. It gives us the ability to play out our circumstances so we can think through our reactions. When we begin to see ourselves as God sees us, then our lives loosen up. We can walk in the freedom that comes with being ourselves. We know our identity. We can quit fighting and start living.

I have a friend who spent months struggling with one of the consequences of divorce: losing the ability to see your kids when you want to. This friend really had a hard time dealing with the decisions their ex-spouse was making. Their ex was making things really hard, and therefore my friend was fighting back with all the power and anger they could muster. I'm talking going toe to toe with lawyers and contempt citations. This went on and on, and the whole time my friend struggled to find any relief.

And then one day they texted me:

I'm thinking about not fighting with them any more.

I thought it was a great idea and told them that, so my friend decided to go through with their plan and stop fighting. And wouldn't you know: my friend got *instant* relief when they made that decision. Why? Because, in my friend's case at least, the fighting wasn't really entirely about seeing the kids – it was mostly about processing the pain of the divorce. When my friend let go of the fight, they were able to let go of the pain they'd been carrying without even knowing it.

Instead of seeing themselves as a divorced person, my friend was able to see themselves as a child of God. They'd found themselves again, and that led to freedom from fear.

Maybe you read that story and you wonder, *But how can you let go? How can you overcome fear to the point where you can let go of it?*

Good question. Let's answer it.

CHAPTER 5

OVERCOME

"The pathway to your greatest potential is straight through your greatest fear." – Craig Groeschel

Not too long ago, there was a viral video going around for a certain carbonated beverage. In this video, an old man introduced as "Uncle Drew" accompanied his nephew to a pick-up basketball game on a public court in New Jersey. The nephew got in a game while Uncle Drew stayed on the sidelines to watch, but when a member of the nephew's team came up with an injury, the young man coaxed his teammates to let Uncle Drew in the game.

Uncle Drew, a paunchy, white-haired and white-bearded, glasses-wearing man in an unfashionable track suit, limped onto the court to disapproving looks from his new team, but his nephew vouched for him and gave him a little pep talk. The game resumed and Uncle Drew played as if he was every bit as rusty and rickety as his outward appearance would lead you to believe.

But then, as the game progressed and Uncle Drew warmed up, he began to hit his shots. He made long three-pointers. He cut through traffic for easy lay-ups. He crossed over defenders and blew by them like they were standing still. He took a fast break back to the other side of the court for a sick jam.

And through all this, crowds gathered on the sidelines and roared with awe every time Uncle Drew did something spectacular. Even those on the court couldn't believe what he was doing.

That's because the old, seemingly broken-down "Uncle Drew" was in reality the young, in-his-prime Kyrie Irving, a number-one draft pick in the NBA and winner of the Rookie of the Year award in 2012. Presumably there were a lot of basketball fans on the court that night, and none of them recognized Irving for the mega-star talent that he is. Why?

Because he was wearing makeup.

Irving didn't go out to the public basketball courts looking like himself – instead, a team of professional makeup artists applied latex, a wig, and imitation facial hair to Irving's youthful appearance to make him look like an old man who was far from his prime.

The same thing can happen to our hope! Hope is always there, but you don't always recognize it because it doesn't always look like you would expect. But that doesn't make it disappear.

The real you is still somewhere in there. You may not see it when you look in the mirror – you may think you look like a rundown, hard-lived old person… but those are just looks.

Your number-one star player is still there. You just can't see it right now.

Or let's look at it this way: a hundred-dollar bill is worth a hundred dollars no matter what condition it's in. It can be crisp and new and so fresh from the bank that it sticks to all the other hundreds in the stack (or so I assume – I'm not used to handling stacks of hundreds). Or it can be rumpled and marked up and stepped on by hundreds of unsuspecting people after it floated down to a sewer grate.

Either way, it's a hundred bucks.

You don't get to decide its value… because a higher authority has already determined how valuable it is, regardless of what you believe about it.

Okay, one more example, just to drive the point home, and I mean that semi-literally, because this example concerns a long-haul truck driver by the name of Teri Horton. Horton, a thrifty woman who was in her seventies at the time this story took place, was in a thrift store in California when she saw an enormous, brightly colored, abstract painting. Finding herself drawn to the colors and thinking the artwork might bring a little joy to a friend of hers who had been dealing with depression, she bought the painting for the price of five dollars.

Unfortunately, the gigantic piece was too large for her friend's house, and ultimately too large for Horton's as well, so she put it out as part of a yard sale, where a local art teacher happened upon it and mentioned to Horton that it resembled the work of legendary abstract painter Jackson Pollock. And if that was indeed the case, then the painting would be worth far more than the five dollars she paid for it. It would be worth about fifty *million* dollars.

Horton took steps to authenticate the painting,

including having a forensics expert match the paint from Horton's canvas with paint that was left as residue in Jackson Pollock's studio. Horton even went so far as to have an expert match a fingerprint found on the artwork with those of Jackson Pollock. In her mind, the evidence overwhelmingly proves that this painting is the real deal.

But not everyone in the art world sees it the same way. Horton wound up having trouble getting the elites of the art market to take her painting seriously, especially since Pollock's style was easily emulated and therefore was copied by numerous other less famous artists. This turn of events made it difficult for Horton to sell the painting, because its value was now being decided by a fickle group of connoisseurs who surely would bristle at the idea of something as brilliant as a Pollock painting being discovered in such a "common" manner by a truck driver who'd never even heard the name Jackson Pollock until after she'd bought his painting.

To Horton, the situation is obvious: whether the elites in control of the market recognize it or not, she is in possession of an undiscovered masterpiece by one of the greatest American painters of the modern era.

In her mind, it doesn't matter what everyone else says

about her painting. She knows the truth.

Much like that painting hiding in plain sight at a thrift store, the tattered hundred-dollar-bill, or like Kyrie Irving hiding his face beneath layers of makeup while flaunting his skill and talent, your true nature is there, inside you, whether you recognize it or not. The hope-filled you, the victorious you, the fearless you, the courageous you.

The real you.

How do I know? Because I speak from experience.

I've always had a pastoral heart. Deep down, I've always been the guy who wanted to help people and see them fulfilled and whole. That's the truth of my heart, the nature God created within me. I get stirred to action and compassion when I encounter the broken and the broken-hearted, when I come across people who are struggling against themselves or against something as insidious as addiction.

Even when I was growing up, I wanted to shepherd those around me and to impart love and care to them. I wanted to do it, but I was afraid of rejection, abandonment, and my own insufficiency. My pastoral part wasn't "cool" among the people I had surrounded myself with in my childhood and adolescence. People would make fun of me for my tenderness and my compassion, and so I started hiding it out of fear until that fear started to look like me. I wore my fear around like Uncle Drew makeup, and I wore it for so long that it became a part of me. It was comfortable. It defined me. It was who I saw when I looked in the mirror.

It became my mask.

I wore that mask for years, adding other layers to it like drugs and alcohol, afraid to take it off but still knowing full well it would have to come off some day.

What's it going to take for you to take off your mask? To peel away the layers of fear and worry that are adding years to your face? For me, it took falling to rock bottom and really coming to grips with who I was, who I'd become, and who I could be. It was about finding the hope and inviting the healing to strip away everything that wasn't really me so that I could at last live free in the nature that God gave me. I could live out my calling, unafraid.

What about you? Maybe you're thinking this sounds really good. Maybe you know you're walking around with your Uncle Drew face but you don't know how to go about taking it off so you can see the real you. Maybe you're scared, too. Maybe you want some change but don't yet have any tools to go get that change or see it happen in your life.

Here are some practical steps you can take to remove that Uncle Drew mask and discover your true self.

Slow Down

One of the main things that can trip us up is when we believe we must act *now*. This is largely a cultural phenomenon, especially in recent years as advertising has become more and more prevalent, telling us we're going to miss out on some incredible deal if we don't sign on the dotted line right this very second.

This is also why you can find candy and soft drinks placed by the checkout line not just at supermarkets but at home improvement warehouses, craft stores, and even some Christian bookstores. The store owners put those there because they know consumers have poor impulse control – they're already at the cash register with their debit cards ready to go, so what's another couple of bucks for a bag of peanut M&M's and a bottle of diet Coke? (I especially don't understand why the Christian bookstores do that – it's not like any Christians act impulsively, right?)

It's all a trick. Most of the stuff that's out there for

impulse purchasing is completely frivolous. You'll be fine if you don't snag that pack of out-of-date gum or five-dollar iTunes gift card. And the same often holds true for the greater things that are bringing pain and fear into your life and holding back your hope.

In the moment, your impulses will tell you that you just need one hit to make it through the day.

In the moment, your impulses will tell you that a quick stop to your favorite porn sites will settle your nerves and calm your racing mind.

In the moment, your impulses will tell you that berating your staff will make you look and feel better.

In the moment, your impulses will tell you that a few extra calories won't throw your diet off track, and besides, you can just run them off later.

In the moment, your impulses will tell you that making fun of someone who is different from you will somehow give you a boost in confidence.

In the moment, your impulses will tell you that a celebratory drink isn't going to ruin your sobriety.

These are all impulses, and if you'll learn to pause and recognize them for what they are, you'll see the hope that comes

90

from slowing down and avoiding impulsive behavior.

Perhaps you're now wondering: are there times when we do in fact need to act on impulse and seize what's in front of us? Absolutely! However, those times are not nearly as frequent as your sin-marinated brain or our advertised-to-the-hilt culture would have you believe. Which is why you need to...

Know Your Stuff

Want to see more hope in your life? Then you need to take an active role in learning about it. One of the best things I ever did for myself was challenging myself to learn more, mostly by reading. You're already doing something for yourself by reading this book; I would encourage you to make reading a habit.

There's something really great about getting outside of yourself and learning about the world around you that helps you slow down and appreciate things – and make better decisions. Find something you're interested in, and then go learn more about it. Maybe you want to know more about the brain science behind drug addiction... learn about it! Maybe you want to know more about the mechanics of a diesel engine... learn about it! Maybe you want to know how the

Bible went from a collection of scrolls and letters in ancient times to the easily searchable app you carry around in your pocket… learn about it! Maybe you want to know how to grow your own strawberries and turn them into homemade preserves… learn about it!

One of the wonderful achievements about the modern world is that you can learn just about anything these days, and usually all it takes is a library card and an Internet connection. Get curious about the world around you and you'll start to see the hope flowing.

And a side benefit of your extended curiosity about other things is that it will both broaden your mindset and deepen your ability to look inward, which is necessary if you're going to…

Recognize Your Problems

We all have problems and we all have tendencies. Every single one of us. And so we must start learning how to recognize those tendencies so we can minimize the negative ones as much as possible and maximize the positive ones.

I think every city has an intersection where traffic accidents happen more frequently, that problem area where, for whatever reason, cars can't seem to avoid each other. And the more it happens, the more the authorities and people in power do to examine the underlying causes behind the collisions and to put safety measures in place to eliminate them. They'll change the speed limit. They'll add a stoplight or a protected left turn. They'll add lanes or remove them.

It's only through recognizing the roots of the problem that they can do anything about it, and the same holds true with us. We have to recognize that we have problems – we have to acknowledge that we can be stubborn, that we can be stupid, that we can be reckless. We have to own up to the fact that we can plunge into stuff without thinking about it and that we feel indestructible at times.

And this act of recognition is a lifelong process. We can't just do it all at once, because we are ever-evolving creatures who understand more and more about ourselves as time goes on; and then, once we understand something, we grow and discover new aspects about ourselves that we then must learn to understand.

I learned this truth firsthand when I went through the heart-rending pain of divorce. Here was a woman I'd pledged myself to, a woman with whom I'd created two wonderful little children. Yes, we got married in a hurry, out of desperation to make an "honest" pregnancy and therefore upping our degree of difficulty for marital longevity, but we were determined to make things work, and there was a lot of love between us.

Unfortunately, my addictions got in the way and I found my relationship with my wife and kids unraveling… and even though it hurt me greatly, I didn't then realize the lasting impact that hurt would have. Because the longer I've been in recovery and the more removed I get from that awful time in my life when my divorce was finalized and my kids were taken out of my world for a time, the greater my ability to see how much that changed me. I know now how deeply that river of pain runs, and I can still identify its effects on my life now. Today.

It changed me. I treat people differently now than I might have before my divorce. I can be much more skeptical in relationships, I can hold people at arm's length instead of letting them in, terrified that I'm going to wind up losing yet another relationship in a devastating way. I can wind up going over the top with that and find myself full of mistrust or doubt about people and their intentions.

I'm finding that this is what happens when I let the pain

of my past weigh me down. If I don't acknowledge that my pain exists and that it's influencing the ways I interact with others, then I'll never be able to change that about myself. Instead, I will let the external circumstances of my divorce worm their way into my head and keep me from fully embracing the future. I won't dream anymore because I'll be too busy reliving the past in my head.

So instead, I have to recognize and acknowledge these things about myself and say, *Okay, I'm going to try to trust someone again. I'm going to put myself out there. I know God's got my back and He isn't going to fail me. Even if I get hurt, I know I'll be okay, the sun will still come up.*

Every time I can take a step back and get a bird's-eye view of myself and the way I'm acting, I can see how those actions are happening as a result of past hurt, past pain, and past shame. And when I can do that, then I can recognize myself for who I've been and who I am now, and that leads to growth. It helps me keep maturing, which in turn gives me hope for the future. This isn't a rainy-day kind of hope or a hope that fades in and out like a dropped phone call – this is grounded, concrete hope.

And look, I understand that taking the mask off can be

really difficult – especially if it's something you've been wearing for years. And the more I've thought about this and talked to other people about it, the more I've realized that so many of us keep wearing the mask because we're afraid to fail. For many of us, the fear of failing becomes so daunting that we never take a step forward to recognize it for what it is. We build up the idea that the world is waiting for us to crash and burn so they can mock us or revel in our humiliation.

But I have good news for you: you aren't that big of a deal! Our minds can play tricks on us, inflating our egos and telling us that everyone is watching us to see what we'll do. But true freedom comes in recognizing that there's only One whose opinion matters, and everyone else is too hung up on themselves to really pay attention to your failures. The world is big and you're ultimately pretty small, meaning you can chase your dreams with little worry for what people think.

How can you develop recognition for who you are? Here are two ideas that I've implemented that have really helped me.

First, *ask for help*. You'll never see yourself for who you are if you can't see the forest for the trees. You have to get a viewpoint from the outside looking in, so ask someone close to you to help you recognize all those trees, name them, identify them, and determine which ones need to be cut down and which ones just need to be plotted around. Then you'll be able to create the roadmap of you.

Give this other person permission to be brutally honest with you and let them provide you with *their experience of you*. Don't retaliate and don't argue – the whole point is to find out how others see you so that you can learn to see yourself. You aren't basing your identity on their opinion anyway, remember?

Second, *take inventory*. Every night as you prepare for bed, think back through the day and track how you managed your fears and processed your pain. Did you wear the mask today? If so, how did it impact you? What can you do differently tomorrow to keep the mask off? Write these things down if you want – it'll probably help you internalize and develop these thoughts.

So there you go. Only after we recognize our problems can we do something about them, and that something we can do is…

Plan, Prepare, Pray, Play

There's a whole book's worth of material for each of these four things, and I encourage you to dig more deeply into the ideas of planning, preparing, praying, and playing. But let's at least talk briefly about each thing.

Planning is the idea of being intentional about your future and about discovering the real you that's lying underneath your Uncle Drew face. Instead of just blindly stumbling around from day to day, planning helps you figure out some goals you want to achieve and puts some purpose to your life, like when Taco Bell decided to make a taco shell out of Nacho Cheese Doritos. That was the plan.

Preparing is the idea of taking those goals and breaking them down into practical, achievable steps with measurable outcomes. Turns out that Nacho Cheese Doritos are made using a totally different process than a Taco Bell taco shell, so the food scientists at the two different companies had to come up with a lot of preparative steps to figure out how to turn one thing into the other. How can they apply the Nacho Cheese powder evenly? How can they ensure the shells don't break in transit between the factory and the restaurant? How can they bake in the familiar Doritos crunch while ensuring the taco shell doesn't shatter into pieces after the first bite? It all required a lot of preparation from a dedicated team of fast food engineers to overcome the challenges and put the plan into practice.

Praying is exactly what it sounds like. All your planning and preparing are worthless if they you don't bathe them in prayer. Marinate them. Soak them. Spray them down with the high-pressured hose that Taco Bell used to distribute that nacho cheese powder on their taco shells. When you blanket your plans and preparations in prayer, you'll be more confident in each step you take, and you'll feel much better about the rare times when you must act on impulse.

Playing is the act of enjoying the Loco Taco you've made! If you want to see how hope can change you, then you have to get out and enjoy life. Quit whining, turn off the TV, and go play. One of the most important aspects of keeping my dream alive today is my laser focus on enjoying life to the fullest. Don't get me wrong – I am often a workaholic, which is a whole other book, but I try to play just as hard as I work. It's a huge part of my recovery and my newfound, hope-filled life.

I try to keep a wide variety of friends and when they want to do something, I make an attempt to practice what I preach and say YES! We have only a limited amount of time in this world and I don't want to waste *any* of it. Now that I have dealt with my past and can proudly claim who I am, it feels good to go out and enjoy life. I don't make excuses for that.

Trust me: when you've been dead for so long, life feels way too good to sit around. You have to sink your teeth into it!

After you've done all this, you can start to…

Forgive

Bitterness is a weight that holds you back and keeps you down. It's an anchor that ties you to your pain and keeps that mask over your face. We haven't really discussed this critical piece of the puzzle yet, but it's so important to learn to forgive.

Your pain may have been inflicted by another person or it may have been the result of your own choices, but either way, you have to forgive. I know it's hard. I know it can feel like giving up or letting the other person win.

I also know that it's necessary for peace, happiness, and hope.

When you forgive, you're acknowledging the power of your pain, you're recognizing what it is doing within you, and you're intentionally cutting off that power in order to get out of that debilitating cycle you're in. Forgiveness brings with it freedom, but sometimes to get there you have to forgive over and over again, probably for the rest of your life.

Now, the good thing is that you don't have to forgive

someone face-to-face, especially if that person has hurt you deeply – sometimes trying to seek them out for a personal act of forgiveness can just lead to more hurt and even danger. Instead, you can do practical things like write them a letter you never mail (burn it instead), or you can type something up for them on the computer and then hit "delete." You can have a friend or loved one stand in for them. If the person you need to forgive is deceased, you might want to plan a trip to their gravesite – I've met with several people who have forgiven this way, and they've found it to be tremendously helpful. If you find you have to forgive yourself, a mirror or even a photograph of your childhood or current self works great (yes, I'm authorizing that selfie!).

The point is: find a tangible way to articulate your forgiveness, and then keep on forgiving, because you'll probably have to.

And then, after all this, you'll finally be able to...

Know Yourself

Who are you? I mean, really: *who are you*? Do you know? Have you ever known? Do you know how awesome, talented, intelligent, and wonderful you are? Do you know how crazy God is about you, and not for anything you do but just because He loves you?

Do you know?

Think about the story of Uncle Drew from earlier. Imagine if, after putting on all that makeup, Kyrie Irving saw himself in the mirror and *believed what he saw*. What if he saw this old man staring back at him and convinced himself that his best days were behind him? What if he forgot his skills and talents and the life-changing career opportunities that lay before him?

What if he looked at the lies caked on his face and fell for them?

What if he forgot who he really was?

Are you doing that?

I believe that, out of everyone in our world, the person we know the least is really ourselves. For a lot of reasons, we just don't know who we are. Some of us are afraid of our true nature, while others of us believe there's nothing there worth knowing.

Either way, it's baloney. The most important person in your life is you. Now, I'm not giving you permission to become a raging narcissist who believes that the world should revolve around them, because that's the opposite swing of this pendulum. But I am telling you that you can't ignore yourself. Your needs, your desires, your hopes and dreams – they all have meaning and should carry weight in your life.

When you know yourself, you can feel comfortable giving yourself time and energy to pursue the things that are important to you. You can feel okay giving yourself opportunities to chase after your dreams, allowing hope to flood your soul and become the fuel for your passions. You can recognize your strengths, but most importantly your weaknesses, and you can begin to set healthy boundaries that enable you to grow securely in your confidence and spirituality.

You probably aren't going to have that mask off in a day. But that doesn't mean you shouldn't at least get started on it! Day by day, little by little, you'll start to peel that mask off and you'll start to see your true self. Maybe it's too hard to pull back a lot of it today – maybe the memories are too fresh or the pain is too deep or the fear of a healthy-but-uncertain future is just too great. That's okay. What can you do today?

Don't stop pushing ahead. Forward motion is good, even if it's barely perceptible. That is when you can overcome your fears and start to move forward in the rest of your life. You can't change your past, but you can live in hope for today, and when you do that, you're taking a stand for the future.

Hope begins now.

CHAPTER 6

YOUR PAIN, YOUR PLATFORM

Each of us walks around with a huge weight around our necks that affects everything about us. The way we walk, the way we talk, the way we see the world. We're limited and slumped over and yet *no one will talk about it*. We refuse to acknowledge that anything is wrong with us, because heaven forbid we seem less than all the other people around us. Instead we'd rather walk around fake and phony, keeping everyone at arm's length while we die inside.

The truth is, everyone has baggage in the closet. *Everyone.* You do, your neighbor does, your boss does, your pastor does, your wife does, and your kids do. Everyone has something. This should be a huge relief to hear. This should bring us all together.

And yet… it doesn't.

So let's change that. Let's embrace the pain we've endured. Let's live in the mess of life and do our best to make it a message. You may not become a sought-after public speaker or evangelize your cause throughout the world, but you can openly embrace what's happened to you and tell it to a friend. Let them in just a bit and see what happens. See if it doesn't change everything about your relationship. See if you don't become closer almost instantly. See if you don't walk away from that conversation with your hearts more aligned. I bet you will.

I made a bold decision early on in my sobriety, one I'm not sure I thought through completely. I certainly didn't have the vision to see what my life would eventually become by making this decision. It felt like the right thing to do, yes, but more than that it felt like what I *had* to do. Almost as if I didn't have a choice.

What was the decision? I chose to live my life as openly and vulnerably as possible, giving everyone I could a front-row seat to the emotions and experiences of a rough and raw recovering drug addict.

What's happened since that choice has been miraculous.

I prayed that God would use my past to make an impact on others but I never thought it would end up like this – especially not writing about it in my second book!

What I found, though, was that the more I opened up about the pain of my past, the more others felt like they were given the permission to do the same. My story is nothing altogether incredible; compared to some of the stories I've heard these past few years, I would say that mine falls in the category of average to good. I know people who have spent years in prison after dealing and using for decades, guys who cooked meth in semi trucks, guys whose only goal was to follow bands around the country for years, women whom God saved literally right off the stripper pole, millionaires who lost it all then changed their lives and got it all back, and then some. I've heard some wild tales since God rescued me.

It's funny how these stories find their way to me. It's not like I set out to ask people about their past or their struggles, but almost as if they can't help but run up and tell me all about it. I think a little has to do with me and a lot has to do with the fact that everyone is searching for a way to offload the pain they've been carrying for so long. I think I've represented transparency and vulnerability to people as I've publicly shared about my past and so people feel like they now have permission to do the same.

Sharing is the first step in how hope changes everything. The more we share about our past, the further from denial we get. And the more others are given the chance to express their story and the pain they've experienced, the closer they come to letting it go.

Fear Snares

The thing about overcoming fears is that they tend to not *stay* overcome. Like pulling weeds from a garden or keeping air in a leaky tire, this is something that requires a little bit of maintenance. Or, to switch to a different metaphor: your fear snares are always going to be out there, so you have to stay on guard and be vigilant to avoid stepping into them in the future.

What do I mean when I say a "fear snare"? I'm talking about anything that binds you emotionally, physically, or spiritually. A snare is anything that reminds you of those fears or pains you've gone to such great lengths to overcome, and when I say anything, I mean *anything*. From certain objects to specific places or regions, from individual people to something as highly unique as a smell or a taste, there are probably more than a few snares out there that take you back to that place where you feel trapped, like you haven't made progress or that stumbling is inevitable.

You'll know these traps not because you see them with your eyes but because you feel them either physically or emotionally, much like a pilot flying blind, using only their instruments. Or, for a more pop-culture style of phrasing, your "spidey sense" will start tingling. If you're from the South and are a little older, you might describe it with the phrase, "You'll know it in your knower."

When it comes to my own snares, I know I'm close to one when I start to lose my appetite, start sweating, or feel anxious. I figured this out when working with a counselor who walked me back through some memories of my past behaviors to find triggers and traps, and we walked all the way back through the ten years of my addiction and right up to that point when I ran out of my parents' living room.

That's when I realized that my first strategic tendency for escaping a trap is to start running. When I get locked up with feelings of rejection, abandonment and failure and feel like I need to bolt, that's when I'm about to run straight into a trap and I need to be most on guard.

My running didn't always look like actual running. When I was a user, I spent so many years just wasting away with no purpose or meaning to my life. I just... existed. Took up space. Consumed air.

It was miserable. I wanted to run, so I did.

I lived with this feeling that I – by myself – was not enough. So my running took the form of perpetually taking something, drinking something, or snorting something to make just about any situation a little "better," a little more "fun," to get a little "higher." And when I say any situation, I mean *any* situation...

Going to a football game? I had to get high to sit out there in the cold.

Making dinner? I had to have a few drinks to get loose.

Sitting down and getting some work done? I had to ease the pressure and smoke a joint.

Going out with friends? I had to get ripped so I could be "myself."

Having my kids for the weekend? I'd better make sure I have enough pills because I'll need the "energy."

Going to church? I better get a little buzzed – I hate having to talk to people sober, plus the light show is so much better.

Going over to see family? I have seven pills in my pocket – that should get me through.

Going to play golf? I'll just tuck a spliff in my cigarette pack for the back nine.

There were really no situations, circumstances, or events I could handle sober. I didn't know how to just be myself. I wasn't very proud of "myself"; I didn't think he had much going on. That guy – "myself" – he was a fake and a phony; a divorced, medicated, bald dependent who was fiercely lonely and horribly afraid. I wanted to run as far from that guy as I could.

We all have our moments where reality just isn't enough. When something deep inside us screams to run away, to flee, or to medicate the painful feelings into submission. Running from challenging feelings and awkward confrontation was second nature to me for so many years.

But here is the bombshell. Here is the truth about me: *I still want to run away today!*

Yes, oftentimes, when I am challenged, when emotions well up inside of me, when people push my buttons, or when life throws me a curve, I still have strong desire to run. To hide.

To medicate. To get stoned. To take some pills.

Truth is, I don't think I'm the only one. In fact, I know I'm not. I spend too much time around people to know that most of us struggle to stay in the moment. It's way too easy nowadays to run away – all we have to do is pick up that phone and instantly we are whisked away to an alternate reality or connected to the dealer of whatever medication gives us a temporary reprieve from ills.

But here is the good news. Since we know that we tend to run, we can stop pretending that we don't! We can vulnerably and honestly look in the mirror and be okay with who we are, and then we can help each other through the difficult times when they arise.

You know what movie I just absolutely love? *The Princess Bride*. From top to bottom and from start to finish, it's just a delightful film. And though it's packed with great scenes from beginning to end, one of my favorites is a scene toward the middle of the film when two of the heroes – Westley, the roguish, devil-may-care pirate who is really out to save his long-lost love, and Buttercup, the plucky "princess bride" of the title (and Westley's long-lost love) who has an equal share in their rescue – are reunited after spending most of the film apart. The couple is being pursued by Prince Humperdinck, who intends to marry Buttercup and then murder her so he can blame it on a neighboring kingdom and start a war, so they dart into the mysterious "Fire Swamp" to hide out.

Buttercup isn't sure about this plan, but Westley, brimming with confidence and derring-do, puts a positive spin on it and keeps a brave face in the midst of a foreboding, overgrown jungle. He cheerfully hacks vines out of the way, creating a path through the underbrush while Buttercup innocently frets.

"We'll never make it out alive," she says.

"Nonsense," replies Westley. "You're only saying that because no one ever has."

If you've seen the movie, you know what happens next – there's a *pop-pop* on the soundtrack and then a huge jet of flame suddenly spews up from the ground, lighting Buttercup's dress on fire. Westley leaps into action and quickly extinguishes the fire, all while maintaining a cavalier smirk on his face.

Crisis averted, they begin to make their way once more through the Fire Swamp when Buttercup takes a bad step and falls right into one of the Swamp's traps: a hole filled with sand that swallows her up in an instant. Thinking quickly once more,

Westley hacks off one end of a long vine, then dives headfirst into the hole after Buttercup, emerging a few agonizing seconds later with her.

Using the vine, they climb out of the hole and back onto the firm ground of the Fire Swamp, and at this point, Buttercup is completely deflated. She is now positive they will never make it out alive and says as much to Westley, who quickly corrects her and runs down "the three dangers of the Fire Swamp." There's the flame spurt, but now they know that, before each spurt, there's a popping sound, which means they can take steps to move out of the way and not be engulfed by the flames. Then there's the lightning sand, about which Westley points out, "You were clever enough to discover what that looks like," meaning they can step around it now that they can identify it.

But then there's the final danger: the R.O.U.S., which stands for Rodent Of Unusual Size. Westley is sure these creatures are just a legend when he is suddenly viciously attacked by one. Of course, this being a fantastical film in the tradition of Saturday matinees, the R.O.U.S. is ridiculously fake-looking, but the threat is real enough in the story, and Westley and Buttercup work together to kill the attacking rodent and make it safely through the Fire Swamp.

So what does this have to do with fear snares? Obviously, there's the surface-level comparison: they had to spot traps in order to get through the Fire Swamp in one piece. That parallel pretty much draws itself. But I want you to notice something else about this story, and that is this: it wasn't enough for them to learn how to identify the snares in the Fire Swamp – they had to defeat them *together*.

If they'd been in there on their own, by themselves, without the other person, they likely would have perished inside the Fire Swamp. Buttercup would've been burned alive by the flame spurt or buried alive by the lightning sand. Westley would likely not have had the strength to fight off the R.O.U.S. without Buttercup's assistance.

The film doesn't show us Westley and Buttercup's complete journey through the Fire Swamp, instead cutting directly from their altercation with the rodent to them emerging from the Fire Swamp, but we can safely assume they spent a little bit of time journeying through to reach the other side. And we can also safely assume that in that time, they were able to point out the traps to each other and help each other through the dangers.

And that's what I'm talking about. Want to keep your

fears at bay? Want to guard your heart? Then you need to have other people walking with you through life. These people can help you identify your fear snares and then help you find some "escape routes" for them -- and maybe even help you to take those escape routes when you need them.

Have you ever driven through the mountains? Oftentimes, the interstates that run through steep mountain passes will have emergency ramps that are placed periodically and strategically, the entire purpose of which is to rescue semi trucks whose brakes have failed due to the steep downward slope. These emergency ramps branch off from the main highway and end in an uphill climb that would slow down even a heavy semi that was speeding downhill.

Now let me ask you this: if the driver of one of those semi trucks loses his brakes, should they take one of these emergency ramps? Should they avail themselves of the escape route, or should they just try to continue controlling a runaway truck using their own white-knuckle determination? Should they steer toward safety or should they let their pride get in the way and say to themselves, "I'm a good driver; I don't need that ramp."

I don't know about you, but if *I* were one of those

drivers, I would take the escape route! Because I know now that I should! There have been times in my past when I would've been cocky about it, thinking I could handle the runaway truck (or even worse – refuse to acknowledge that the truck had even gotten away from me), but now I know better. I know that I need to take the escape routes that I've designated for myself. And my Hope Partners, as I call them, help me do just that.

Like that mountain drive, the journey of life will sometimes be a pleasant detour that you can enjoy with minimal distractions or obstacles, and sometimes it will be like a treacherous trek through the Fire Swamp with traps close at hand that require vigilance. Either way, it's best to have one or two people walking along beside you, accountability partners (or Hope Partners) who can help you stay on track and for whom you can do the same.

You can't do this on your own, and you shouldn't try. Because accountability requires much more than just a desire to live right – it requires a certain amount of humility that can sometimes be difficult to come by (for a full and thorough discussion on the importance of Hope Partners in your life, please see Chapter Five of my book *Hope Is Alive*).

I've been sober for a long time, but I still occasionally

get looks from my friends and family or other people close to me that can be interpreted in no way other than this: "Are you high, Lance?" Sometimes people even come right out and ask me if I've been using, and I'll be honest, it often triggers some quick anger from deep within myself. Like, I'm offended that they would even think such a thing! I mean, it's not like I buried myself in drugs and alcohol for a solid decade, destroying everything and everyone close to me in the process and completely wrecking my life!

Oh, wait. Whoops.

I've found that this reflexive, "How could you even *ask* such a thing?" attitude is common among recovering addicts, at least among the ones I know, anyway, and I think I know why. See, simply managing to string together a few days of sobriety is a huge success for us, and once we get a few of those in a row, we get excited enough to forget all the pain and hurt we caused during that long, long stretch of not-so-clean days. We get selective about what we want to remember and what we want to forget, and we're so grateful for these great new memories that we tend to let go of the bad ones and cherish the good ones.

Now, in some ways this can be a good practice, but it does apply to accountability in a way. Because we can start to think of accountability as the other person's responsibility, putting the weight on the shoulders of our accountability partner, the one who has to occasionally ask us: "Are you high right now?," we can sometimes forget that we have to own accountability for ourselves just as much.

So what are some ways we can embrace our role in the accountability relationship? I'm glad you asked! Let's look at just three:

Own It

How did you get that Hope Partner in the first place? You asked them, right? Of course you did (unless a judge assigned you a mentor or sponsor, in which case you're in a totally different situation, but still one that requires a lot of work – and where your sobriety has a lot on the line). But that relationship only comes about because you asked someone into your life. You gave them permission to question you, critique you, and check on you.

So since you gave them that permission, you need to own it! Own your accountability and don't get defensive or chop them down at their knees when they ask questions that might feel a little personal or that you feel uncomfortable answering.

But guess what? It's very difficult to hold someone accountable! If you've ever done it, you know exactly what I mean. It can be very tough to put yourself into someone else's business, even when they've given you the permission to do it. And it can get even tougher when the person who asked for accountability in the first place doesn't own up to their part of the bargain.

Part of my job as an accountability partner to the addicts I work with at Hope HQ involves doing some pretty difficult stuff. I have to ask tough questions, double-check people's work, and care enough to call the guys out when they aren't owning their sobriety, and it's probably the hardest part of my job. I guess there are a few people in this world who really dig bossing others around, but my experience is that most of us find it a less than enjoyable to hold someone's feet to the fire like this, especially in the type of accountability relationship that I have with these men.

It isn't easy, but it's ultimately rewarding when I remember all the times others have done the same thing for me, and the times when I get to be vulnerable with these guys and let them into my world a little bit. But the moment any of us tries to get all huffy and puffy about a question we didn't like, we do our best to remember as quickly as possible that we *asked* for this accountability in the first place, so we need to own it.

Confront It

I wear a lot of different hats in life. I'm a speaker, an author, a project manager, a marketer, a counselor, a blogger, a consultant, a fundraiser, a father, and many other things. But out of all the things I do in a typical week, the most challenging task I face each and every day is attempting to mentor the five men living in my recovery house, which I call Hope HQ. (If you don't know, the non-profit I founded – Hope Is Alive Ministries – operates a recovery house for men in Oklahoma City who are getting their lives back on track after getting out of rehab. I live there and run all the rest of my gigs from an office in the back.) The five guys I live with are a part of a program that provides them opportunities to take their lives to the next level professionally, spiritually, emotionally, physically, and relationally.

The day-to-day mentoring, accountability, and leadership of these unbelievable guys is probably the hardest thing I've ever done. Why? Not because the guys are consistently out of line or messy (well... maybe) or deliberately breaking rules. On the contrary, they work hard on their programs, chase after goals, help others, serve at churches, and do it all while having a blast.

No, what makes this job so tough is the fine line I must walk between mentorship and friendship. Because somewhere between these two things lies a word that many of us shy away from. It scares us, causes us to be uncomfortable, lose our appetite and start sweating. It can be a nasty word that evokes fear and doubt deep within us. In fact, it's the word I'm most afraid of…

Confrontation.

Life is always going to put things in your path that can distract you or derail you or whatever, and when it does, you have a choice to either confront it or cower from it. There are no other options.

Think about it in your workplace. Do you ever face confrontation?

What about your home, with your spouse or children?

What about those of you who are dealing with kids struggling with addiction? How hard is confrontation for you?

It's tough, right? It's very challenging, and that's why this job is the hardest job I've ever had.

But it's also why it's the most rewarding. Why?

A popular verse in Proverbs talks about mentoring and friendship, saying: "As iron sharpens iron, so one person sharpens another." (Proverbs 27:17) But what this verse doesn't say is that when iron strikes iron, oftentimes sparks fly! And let me tell you – sparks can fly around this house.

This type of combustible atmosphere is what makes this job so challenging. It's also what makes accountability, raising children, leading people and helping a loved one in denial so difficult. But red hot confrontation is also what makes this environment and these relationships so conducive to growth. You see when sparks fly, they typically produce a fire, and although fire can be something that can destroy, it's also something that produces new life, change, purification, and growth. It makes some things moldable and shapeable so they can be fastened into something greater and sharper than just their raw material would suggest.

The fire of confrontation leads to minor, healthy explosions. When you watch a fire closely, you see dozens of tiny explosions taking place. Pockets of air, gas, and flammable materials are all responding to the flame and setting off chemical reactions. The same things happen within a *well-constructed* confrontation.

It's important to understand the difference between confrontation and argument, by the way. In a confrontation, both parties are expressing themselves and are most likely doing so freely. This is good. We need to let off steam sometimes. And as long as neither party gets too personal or malicious, then things are okay.

These therapeutic explosions allow people to finally express themselves and feel as if they are being heard. Explosions are often fueled by days', months', or even years' worth of baggage coming to the surface all at once – so no wonder it sometimes seems as if it's *spewing* out like a volcano. I encourage this to take place, because the more negativity you are able to get out, the more positivity you can pour back in. So when you confront someone, allow them to express themselves explosively if they must. Let them get it out and then, if you need to express yourself, go right ahead. Politely, of course.

Oftentimes confrontation can come about as a result of misinformation and misinterpretations. But even then, it's good! What happens when two people finally sit down to hash things out is this: the truth inevitably comes to the surface and the facts of the matter are found out by both parties. What really happened, how it made them feel, how it made you feel, who it hurt, what was really said, the meaning behind the words, the intention behind the action. Through confrontation, I can quickly see and hear the true story and determine where I might have been wrong in the matter. If this happens to you, then you need to promptly admit your fault and seek forgiveness; if it happens to the Hope Partner you're confronting, then graciously accept their apology.

I've also found that within every difficult confrontation I've had to make, there's always this magical moment when someone hears something for the first time. Now, they may have heard the same words or phrasing or story in the past, but there is something about a confrontation that bolsters your listening skills. Our senses are raised, our emotions are on point, and we are finally able to understand something we've been missing for months. Our perspective begins to change, because we've allowed ourselves – for probably the first time – to see things from a different angle. Taking in someone else's experiences gives us understanding unavailable to us before.

It's the beauty of confrontation.

You may be facing a confrontation yourself. You know it's coming and are running scared, doing anything you can to avoid it. But let me encourage you to face what's in front of you, because there's a reward on the other side of that confrontation. The fire you must walk through will produce new life in both you and your Hope Partner.

Face It

Don't play hide and seek with your Hope Partner. I've seen this time and again – someone gets turned on to the idea of accountability and jumps in wholeheartedly, with both feet, getting set up with an accountability partner or two and attacking the whole concept like a police dog on a suspect.

And then the newness wears off and what happens? Suddenly they start to slip a little in their behavior and start to miss meetings as a result. They don't want to talk about how they took a couple days off from going to the gym or how they haven't been reading their Bible every night, and so they start hiding out from the person they specifically asked to help keep them in line. They let phone calls go to voicemail and pretend to ignore texts, and before long they're ducking out the back door at church or hiding behind endcaps at Wal-Mart just so they don't get seen.

It doesn't have to be this way. It *shouldn't* be this way!

If you feel like you have to dodge your Hope Partner, my first question would be: why? Do you feel like this person is here to judge you or guilt you into submission? I promise they probably aren't! If you do get that vibe from them, then please talk to them about it and make sure they understand where you're coming from, how you feel, and what you need.

This person is in your life to support and encourage you, and hopefully you're there to do the same thing. They aren't your judge – they're your advocate! So if you do fall off your proverbial wagon, just face the fear head-on, call up your accountability partner, and tell them what happened. Tell them you blew it, that you messed up, that you did whatever, but that you're ready to get back on track. They'll understand, and they'll be proud of you for stepping up like that. This type of direct responses cuts through any potential tension and lets both of you find middle ground once more to get back on track toward success.

And most importantly, *be* the type of accountability partner that you want, and you'll start to see a huge turnaround. Best of all, you'll start to live a lifestyle of overcoming your fear. Once you've figured *that much* out, then you'll be able to look down the road of your life and start to gain a new vision for it. And that's what we're going to talk about next.

CHAPTER 7

PERMISSION TO DREAM AGAIN

It was freezing outside and the rain had started picking up, so I was sort of half-jogging to my car when I heard some foot steps behind me. I quickly turned around to discover a young man following me to my car. Wondering what was going on and whether this guy needed help or I was about to need it, my eyes immediately met his and I got my answer. He was on the brink of breaking down.

I stopped, letting the chill rain soak into my jacket and bounce off my head and the man – barely older than a boy, actually – inched closer toward me. He stuck out a fist and pushed a crumpled wad of cash into my hand, then looked me in the eyes and said, "This is the last four dollars I have. Can I get one of your books?"

Let me back up.

I had just given a talk at a treatment center in Oklahoma. I'd shared my story to a small group of men who were currently in treatment for addiction, and then I shared about dreams. I told these men about the remarkable dreams I began to have for myself while I was in treatment, just like they were right then. I told them how I took advantage of that time and began to dream of a new life, full of hope and freedom.

My dream was simple at first, really consisting of a life filled with real friendships, honest relationships, and with no more shame or guilt but rather passion-filled inspiration. My dream left me smiling at the end of every day and gave my time in treatment a purpose and a goal.

I then talked about how my dreams motivated me, encouraged me, and inspired me to keep pushing ahead. In fact, my dreams were one of the things that helped me do the hard work that was a part of my treatment, and I began to realize while I was there that even though my dreams from the past had sometimes failed or flopped, that didn't mean I had to stop dreaming.

I told them that the same thing would hold true for

them, that if they could start to dream again, they would find amazing things within themselves and also discover that God had incredible designs for their futures. But I wanted to leave them with one thing.

I wanted them to understand that they had permission to dream again.

So many of us are afraid to dream. We start off as dreamers in childhood, and then, little by little, life disappoints us time and again, and we see dream after dream after dream die in front of our eyes. It can make us a little afraid to dream anymore, and so we stop, settling instead for whatever life might hand out to us.

I wanted these guys to understand that didn't have to be the case. That we can keep dreaming.

We just need to give ourselves permission.

After I finished my little talk, a few of the guys stuck around in the meeting room to shake my hand and talk a bit about their past, their story, how they wound up in a treatment center, and what kinds of dreams they might start having for their lives once more. It was a nice time, but I was more than exhausted and ready to take a break when the time finally came for me to pack up my stuff and head back to my car. The cold weather and almost-freezing rain only added to my desire to get back home, crank the heater, and watch an inspiring movie.

And that's when this guy stopped me and tried to exchange all the money he had for a copy of my book. I looked back and forth between those crumpled bills and the young man's rumpled exterior, and my stomach fell in compassion for him. His eyes were pleading with me, saying, *Please, Lance... I need this.*

Stunned, I took a step toward my car, opened the trunk to pack my stuff away, and got out a book. It was a brand new feeling of insignificance as I looked at that compendium of my meager words, knowing that this man was placing so much value on them. I handed it to him and muttered something about just taking it.

He refused. "No, I want to pay you for it," he said. "I haven't dreamed in years, and what you said... well, it really moved me." He took the book and made sure I got the money. "I guess I just needed permission."

By this point, the rain was no longer the only thing soaking his cheeks, and I was doing my best to maintain my composure and keep my own tears at bay, so I just gave him a hug instead of trying to invent any words of wisdom. None were coming to me anyway. The best thing I could say was something I'd already said in my talk:

"Today's the day you can start dreaming again."

And that was it. Before that night, this guy didn't know me from Adam, and he may *still* not know anything about me or even remember who I am. But I like to think that he took that permission to dream and did something with it. Maybe he started dreaming of a new version of himself, of a forever-changed life, of a world where...

- His family is reunited

- He has a new job

- He lives a life free from the insanity of addition

- He's the dad he always wanted to be

- His parents are proud of him again

- He is successful, appreciated and respect by his peers

- He has friends and is valued

- He is married to the woman of his dreams...

Dreams change everything.

Emotions and passions that used to lay dormant inside

you spring up to life, with a dream.

Impossible thoughts begin to become possible again, with a dream.

Journeys and experiences that you thought could never be obtained become conceivable, with a dream.

Depressed, lonely nights grow to echoes of laughter and the chatter of friendship, with a dream.

Hopeless situations and relationships blossom into rewarding and satisfying connections, with a dream.

A life perfectly crafted for you can be obtained, with a dream.

Ideas tossed aside for years transform into world-changing solutions, with a dream.

Your story begins to change people's lives, with a dream.

Dreaming is hope put into action in your thoughts and in your desires for the future, and hope changes everything.

Wherever you are today, whatever it is you are up against, whether you're stuck in a disappointing relationship, struggling to believe you'll ever get clean or trying to understand what it is you're supposed to be doing with your life – today is the day it can all change.

Right now, in this sentence, I am giving you permission

to dream again.

God's giving you permission to dream again.

There. You have it.

So take a moment and think of the life you've always wanted... I'm not going anywhere.

What does that life look like?

What does it sound like?

Where are you?

Who is there with you?

What are you doing?

Whatever it is, I believe you can get there... but it starts with a dream.

No matter what you've done in your life, no matter how old you are or where you started from, you can always dream. Maybe you've had a life of shattered dreams and are finding it difficult to start over, or maybe you're still young and vibrant. Either way, your dreams await you. There's never a time to stop dreaming.

Dreams spring from hope. Hope is the soil you plant your dreams in, the seasoned and fragrant logs that fuel the fire of your dreams.

And hope changes everything.

CHAPTER 8

THE GIFTS GOD HAS GIVEN YOU

When you're looking for hope in the Bible, there are plenty of verses to be found. However, in the midst of a search for hope, it seems a little odd to turn to a book called "Lamentations," doesn't it? And yet, there it is, only three chapters into it:

"The faithful love of the Lord never ends! His mercies never cease. Great is his faithfulness; his mercies begin afresh each morning. I say to myself, 'The Lord is my inheritance; therefore I will hope in him.'" (Lamentations 3:22-24, NLT) I love the affirmation this scripture provides us: every day is a day when God refreshes His mercies toward us! No matter what has happened in the past, God's mercies are new today. Even if *today itself* is a crappy day, we can be assured that tomorrow is a new day, and yet another opportunity for God to do something fresh and faithful in our lives.

One thing I've learned about God the longer I've walked with Him is that he is a good Father who takes care of his kids. He has given each of us gifts that we can use to expand His kingdom and through which we can worship Him. But most of all, He's given each of us exactly what we need for *today*.

This is especially useful when you feel short of hope, because it frees you up from feeling like you have to manufacture your own hopes for the future. If you have some, great! If not, no worries – God will give them to you. But most of all, He'll give you hope for this day, this moment in time.

God loves to give us what we need, when we need it – even when we don't seem very grateful for it in the process. Want to get a closer look at what I mean? Let's take a look at the book of Exodus and I think you'll understand.

Exodus tells the story of the Israelites as they leave their enslavement in the land of Egypt and head out to the promised land. You probably know the part about the plagues, how Pharaoh finally lets them go, how God parts the Red Sea so the Israelites can cross on dry land. They were finally free… to wander around in the desert.

And that's where their gratitude at freedom wore out and their grumbling set in. In Exodus 16:3, we read their complaint to Moses and Aaron: "If only we had died by the Lord's hand in Egypt! There we sat around pots of meat and ate all the food we wanted, but you have brought us out into this desert to starve this entire assembly to death."

Since we know the Israelites eventually make it to the Promised Land, it's easy to criticize the Israelites both for their ingratitude and for their nostalgically wistful thinking about their time in Egypt. However, I don't know about you, but I can identify. I've had marked moments in my own life where I felt like I was in a wilderness, and all I could do was shake my fist at God and say, "Why?"

When I first got sober, while I was still in treatment, I felt God call me into this line of work one night. I remember it clearly: I was so incredibly grateful for my sobriety – it was such a new, refreshing thing to feel healthy once more, and I was practically overwhelmed by how wonderful it all was – and I was literally on my knees thanking God for it. For this new life that He had been so instrumental in providing for me. For this second chance at freedom that I had been given, even though I didn't feel like I deserved it.

I'd never tasted this kind of freedom before in my life, even before I started using, and I found it incredibly humbling. So there I was, thanking God for it, when I heard Him clearly speak to my heart and say, *Lance, I've called you to make an impact in the lives of the broken and the hurting.*

That was all it took. I began to recalibrate my hopes and dreams toward fulfilling that call, setting off to do what God had put in front of me to do, but not really knowing how it would come about. Within a few months of leaving treatment and going back to my old job, I got an opportunity to return to that treatment center. But instead of going as a patient, this time I would go as an employee.

I leapt at the chance. I was working at a family business, for a stable company I would likely inherit one day, and from the outside, it looked like a great job for a guy like me. But it had nothing to do with that call. Instead, I felt like it was time to give up all that stability and head into a new phase of my life with this new job opportunity. So I took the job at the treatment center and never looked back.

Those first few months, it sure felt like God was fulfilling that call He'd given me that night on my knees. The longer I worked there, the more that call felt solidified in my heart. It was everything I could've imagined or hoped for at the time; I loved working with addicts and their families, watching these guys' lives change little by little every day, seeing miracles happen right in front of my eyes. Every day was an inspiration.

The job itself was a perfect fit, blending together my business skills and marketing ability, along with the opportunity to lean on my story daily in order to offer hope to others and to find strength for myself. On top of that, I was living out my passion right in the middle of all this. It was great!

And it suddenly, without warning, it came to an abrupt end.

I had no notice. I wasn't expecting it.

They just didn't need me anymore.

I was absolutely crushed. Outside of my addiction, this time is the lowest point of my life. I was devastated for days, hardly able to get out of bed or get a bite to eat. I was paralyzed with a complex cocktail of emotions that I couldn't even process fully. I was humiliated because I'd put myself out there, had left a lucrative and stable job in order to do this, and now I felt lost. Wandering in the wilderness.

I was angry. Upset. I cried out to God, just like the

Israelites did. "Why?!" I cried out. "Why did You lead me out of that safe job and into this new one, only to take it away from me?! You promised me this! Now what am I going to do?!"

Just like the Israelites, I could only see the wilderness.

Let's go back to that wilderness, where the Israelites were complaining to Moses about the wonderful food they had in Egypt, asking him how they were going to eat. Notice that God didn't wait for the Israelites to clean up their hearts before He starts to take care of them. In the very next verse, God lays out his instructions – He's going to give them some food. And He's going to do it in a fantastic way.

"I will rain down bread from heaven for you," He says.

And that's exactly what God does, sending a sort of bread that the Israelites wind up calling *manna* (which, incidentally, is a sort-of word that sounds much like the Hebrew phrase "What is it?"). This manna is apparently an ancient super-food, because it takes care of all the dietary and nutritional needs of the Israelites for the next forty years.

The guidelines God gives about the manna are my favorite, though. He tells them it's going to appear every morning and they need to gather up what they need for the day. And just to make sure it's fair, He supernaturally prohibits hoarding, which we read in Exodus 16:17-18: "The Israelites did as they were told; some gathered much, some little. And when they measured it by the omer, the one who gathered much did not have too much, and the one who gathered little did not have too little. Everyone had gathered just as much as they needed."

So they have enough food for the day, and God specifically tells them not to try to keep any of it overnight. Then Moses reiterates this. And while many of them heeded the words of God and Moses, some of them decided to do their own thing, and you know what happened? The manna went bad overnight! Specifically, "it was full of maggots and began to smell" (Exodus 16:20).

God gave them exactly what they needed for the day.

He'll do the same for you.

You may not realize this, but God believes in you. He loves you and thinks you're worth His time and attention. He wants you to dream, but He also wants to be the author of those dreams.

There's a psalm that a lot of Christians love to quote as evidence that whatever thought pops into their head was given to them by God. The particular verse is Psalms 37:4, "Take delight in the Lord and he will give you the desires of your heart." A lot of Christians read this and take it to mean that, since they have a fleeting desire to marry someone wealthy or win a Super Bowl or become a beloved music icon to millions of people, if they just quote that verse enough, then God will give that to them. After all, it says He'll give you the desires of your heart, right?

Not so fast.

What if we've misinterpreted that? What if it really means that God will *place His desires within your heart*? Think of the implications! This way, when you submit yourself to Him, He gives you dreams that line up perfectly with the gifts you have.

When I was a kid, I had a dream to play in the NBA, but my height and other limitations of my game were never going to allow me to do that. I'd be fine as a basketball player in junior high and high school, and maybe if I'd gone to college. But to play in the NBA? It wasn't going to happen.

Because those weren't the gifts that God gave me.

He gave me gifts of empathy and compassion. He gave me gifts of speaking truth to the broken-hearted. He gave me a genuine love for the hurting and the outcasts. And He's given me dreams in all those areas, dreams that line up perfectly with my gifts.

Further, He's given me experiences that prepared me to take my pain and my passion and turn them over to Him so He can produce something great from it. It's no coincidence that I grew up in the ministry and saw the church world from the inside out. I had the pleasure of seeing my dad walk through life as one of the most incredibly giving, kindhearted, and encouraging men I've ever seen – and I watched it from the front-row pew.

God opened up doors in business while I was still relatively young; I learned how to communicate and work with people older than me. Shoot, I sold my first car at the age of 16.

God put mentors in my life all along the way and gave me incredible experience… and then I walked through addiction, judgment, ridicule, brokenness, and humiliation.

You see where I am going with this?

God took all of my past experiences, talents, pains and rolled them out into a dream life I couldn't have written for myself if I'd tried. Today I don't work – I *live*. I don't feel the pressure to be anyone else, because God has me doing what He wants me to do.

And the same holds true for you. Your past, your skills and your passions line up, and the equal a dream life you may have never imagined.

So what are your gifts? When you dream, do your dreams involve those gifts being put into practice? Don't sell yourself short in answering these questions, either. It's okay to acknowledge your strengths and areas of your life where you have obvious giftings. You can do that and still be humble.

Still not sure what your gifts might be? Crowdsource the information. Ask five people who know you well what gifts they see in you. Listen to what they say and take it in. I know it can sometimes be uncomfortable to hear people brag about you, but you need to get over that and accept yourself for who you are, both for your flaws and for your positive attributes.

Your gifts may not be obvious to you or they may not immediately look like they could be a big deal in God's kingdom. So what?! If God's given you something, it matters to Him! If your gift lies in hospitality or taking care of your kids, that's great! If it's in tax preparation, that's awesome! You have something to give to this world on behalf of your Creator, you just must recognize it and then ask God for ways to put it into action.

CHAPTER 9

HOPE CHANGES EVERYTHING

While I was in the midst of writing the first draft of this book, I was able to reconnect with an acquaintance from my past. I still have a lot of work left to do in restoring the damage I've caused throughout my life, and this person was one of the many, many people that I unknowingly and unwittingly tore down through my destructive behavior in adolescence.

They contacted me through Facebook and, after we exchanged some pleasantries and got caught up on all the relevant spouse/kids/career info, they asked me a simple question: "What as a person did I do to you and your friends to deserve the way I was treated?"

Well, while I can't say I was exactly shocked at the

question – after all, I've had to answer this kind of question quite a few times as I've worked through my recovery – I was sort of shocked at how quickly it came up, and how bold and open they were in asking it.

I apologized and asked for forgiveness, which I received, and then we started digging a little more deeply into their situation, and I was floored by their honesty and bravery:

"My life was so awful, Lance, I had to drop away from everyone and everything. I worked full-time and took care of my then-alcoholic father. Nothing like coming home from work and finding your father throwing up blood on your bathroom floor. I knew all the while that there was more to life. I lived through a divorce, molestation, and [sexual abuse] as a young adult. And that was just a part of it. [But] I understood more about the people around me than they did. I have forgiven. Forgetting is the hard part."

So much pain wrapped up in just a paragraph. They then told me they were on their second marriage and that the sexual abuse they'd experienced as a young person was still wreaking havoc on them. "I feel like I am dirty," they wrote. "Unclean and unable to love with all that I am… I feel like I am limiting my spouse. Or somehow cheating them out of the love they deserve."

I asked them about the specific ways they've managed to come to terms with their pain, and this was their response: "I didn't come to terms with my pain, meaning that I didn't accept it. I have confronted the people that have hurt me… I have gotten consumed by my pain at times. I have been dragged down. I can't say I was always strong. After my divorce, I was diagnosed with PTSD, and I've never been in an actual war. But I was going through an emotional war. And was losing the battle.

"[But] I knew that one day someone in my life would love me. I have my [spouse] and my kids, and they love me. I have learned to talk about the bad in my life. Locking it up was killing me. I try my best to forgive, but the sadness is still there. Inside I am still a child waiting for [their] protector."

I can relate, because sometimes I, too, feel completely lost.

In fact, this hollow emotion hits me probably twice a day at least. For a moment, the future looks impossibly hard to navigate, hope seems to be lost, and lifelong sobriety seems way out of reach.

But what's worst of all is that, when this emotion hits

my heart, I feel like I'm all alone, like no one else on earth could possibly feel the way I do. Everyone else seems to know where they're going and who they're going with. All you have to do is check Facebook or Instagram and you'll see joy, purpose, happiness, passion. Everyone seems to have what they want or they're headed across town to get it. And then there's *me*.

Why don't I have what they have?

Where are my celebrity pictures and courtside seats?

I should have a model girlfriend and a new car. Right? So why don't I?

Are they working harder than me?

What do I have to do to live that life?

What's wrong with me?

Sometimes I just feel lost....

Do you ever this feel way? I know I can't be the only one, right?

A few years back I was facing another big prevailing problem in my life: sobriety. And back then I thought I was the only one staring down that demon as well. Turns out I wasn't. A beautiful little ranch out in Oklahoma showed me that at least thirty other men were struggling with the same problem. That tiny little revelation that other people were struggling with the same problems that I was struggling with changed my life forever. I realized I was not alone and that gave me hope. *And that hope changed everything.*

Hope told me I wasn't alone, but that I was surrounded by people just like me.

Hope gave me a future when all I could see was pills and booze.

Hope gave me the confidence to say yes to new opportunities.

Hope gave me a purpose when I lived in apathy.

Hope showed me a world I didn't know existed.

Hope gave me the ability to love myself.

Hope inspired me to get back out there.

Hope made a platform from my pain.

Hope freed me when I was imprisoned.

Hope taught me to care for others.

Hope found me when I was lost.

Hope changed everything!

I can remember the first time I sat in group therapy and listened to other men share their stories. I couldn't sit still, I was practically bouncing up and down, saying to myself, *"Yes, I did that!"* and *"Yep, I do that too!"* Crazy story after crazy story hit so close to home I could practically hear the doorbell ringing. I walked out of that first session feeling ten pounds lighter, holding my head up for the first time in nearly ten years. Why? Because I'd just found out that I wasn't alone after all.

So if I wasn't alone *then*, I know that I am not alone *today*. And that gives me hope.

That's why I found so much hope in what my friend was writing to me on Facebook as I was writing this book. I want to share one more quote they had for me:

"For awhile I was having a rough time emotionally. I told my [spouse] it was time for me to let go of the darkness inside, because I need to know happiness. I need to be able to smile because my heart isn't heavy and full of resentment, pain, and tortured emotions. I have given pain enough of my life. I am not giving it anymore."

As you've gone through this book, my hope is that you too have found some relief in knowing that other people are struggling too. You are not alone! What you see on social media is just the highlight reel of people's lives, and even then it's not always reality. We live in a world that tells us to show our best and hide the rest.

The fact is, Michael Stipe was right on back in 1996:

everybody *does* hurt. We do feel lonely and filled with doubt, sometimes. But the quickest way to take a step back towards joy and happiness is accepting that you are not alone.

We are walking this journey hand in hand. You've got my back and I've got yours. Together we can do this. And when we can come to believe in this sacred hope, then everything begins to change.

I believe in Jesus and all He said and did, which means I also believe what He said in Matthew 11:30 about living a life with Him. He said, "My yoke is easy and my burden is light." Not hard, not heavy. Easy and light.

How? Because Jesus is the new way, the new life, and He came to say it's not about the old way, it's not about the rules, rituals, and regulations – it's about a right-standing relationship.

When I'm off track, His love guides me back.

When my thoughts get ahead of me, His wisdom slows me down.

When I'm nervous about the future, He reminds that He is my hope and that He has plans to prosper me, not to harm.

When I'm scared, I can trust that He is more powerful and let Him whisper in my ear, *Fear not, my son, for I have overcome the world!*

With this confidence I go running towards the future, my head held high knowing there is nothing I cannot do, no person who could ever stop me, no mountain too high, no valley too low, for my God is the ultimate hope – and when we grab on to his hope it changes everything!

Hope grows inside of you each day you choose to get up and decide once more to live in the solution. I am going to live in the promise that God has given me – will you? With each step you take the hope inside you builds; you step away from fear and doubt and step toward the balance and synergy you've always longed for.

Hope never drops you off at a final destination, leaving you with a sign that says *I'm finished, I'm healed.* No, hope moves through you as you move through life. And that's the way you want it. Grasping the concept that the hope inside you can only grow and build throughout your life should move you passionately and give you a comfort and contentment that before has been unattainable.

When you find hope, it changes you. Not your outside, but your inside. It changes your heart, it sands off the rust and pain that's built up over years and years of living in the fear and pain of the past.

Hope is when you start to believe God has given you the greatest gift of all, the gift of grace, and that His love for you will never change. Nothing you do will make Him love you more and nothing you do will make him love you less.

This is how awesome God is: He's walked with you through your entire journey. Even the times when you didn't want Him there, he was around. He's experienced the pain, watched as you've wrestled and toiled with the heartache and fear that follows, and even when the pain drove you to run further and faster away from his gracious grip, He kept pursuing you.

You see, God's grace is a force you can't stop – He's coming after you whether you like it or not. But He won't chase you down with finger wagging, asking, *How could you have done this to Me?* Instead, He comes to you with a smile on his face, begging for you just to come home.

This talk of coming home reminds me, of course, of the parable of the prodigal son that Jesus tells in Luke 15:11-32. You probably already know it, since the term "the prodigal" is already a widespread part of our vocabulary. You probably already know that it's a parable Jesus told about an irresponsible son who demanded his inheritance early, got it, then left home and lived irresponsibly, blowing the money on carousing and revelry, the pleasures of the flesh.

He was able to spend himself into oblivion until he was starving and dreaming about eating pig slop. He decided to go back home in the hopes of getting a job just working on his father's estate – he's hoping to become a hired hand. The parable concludes with the son coming back home and the father jumping for joy over it, embracing him, and restoring him to his place not as a hired hand but as a son (and then the *other* son getting all sulky about it).

What I love about this story is not only that hope changed everything for that son, but that the father completely blew his mind about it. The son, having dishonored his father and blown all his money, got just a sliver of hope into his brain – *maybe I can go home and at least be a servant.* That small amount of hope gave him enough strength to get his eyes off himself and turned back toward home – it became a driver for him, giving him enough strength to somehow make the journey back to where his father lived.

His hope was the motivating factor, but the great thing about God is that He sees our small amounts of hope and is so pleased at the effort that He douses us in more hope than we could've ever imagined for ourselves in the first place (see Ephesians 3:20 for more on this).

My hope – and it is now a big one – is that you're feeling inspired enough to find your *own* hope now. I started off this book by talking about the death of dreams, especially my own. But what about you? What kinds of dreams have you had, and how have they died? Are you able to hope for them again? Are you capable of hoping that they would be resurrected?

Can you hope for a miracle?

In John Chapter 11 we read a great story about people who had given up on something, even in the midst of Jesus looking them in the face and telling them otherwise. The thing they'd given up on? A guy named Lazarus.

He was dead. He'd been dead for four days, actually. And now Jesus was at his house talking with this family, and Lazarus's family kept telling Jesus, essentially, "What's the deal? Why weren't You here? If You'd been here, he wouldn't be dead!"

They weren't prepared for what Jesus was going to do, but he reassured them that it was okay. All they needed was enough hope to obey him when he told them to open up Lazarus's grave by rolling the stone out of the way.

And then Jesus says the simple words: "Lazarus, come out!"

Boom. The dead man wakes up and walks out.

In that moment, Jesus looked death in the face and essentially said, "You can't tell me what to do. You don't own me. You are not the final answer – *I am*. You don't get the last word – *I do*."

Jesus still feels the same way about you. About your dreams.

Your pain doesn't get the last word.

Your past doesn't get it either.

Jesus does.

He wants to resurrect you. He wants to resurrect your dreams, to breathe life into them again, to pump lifeblood once more through those veins.

I imagine that Lazarus had a pretty interesting life after that day. Because no matter how hard things got for him, he could always say to himself, "You know, this has been a pretty cruddy day, but at least I'm alive. After all, I used to be dead!"

I imagine that Lazarus was able to use that quite a bit. I imagine that, wherever he went, he told the story of how he died, and was buried, and how Jesus woke him up and called him out of the grave. His presence alone was a reminder of God's miracle-working ability to transform something intensely painful – death – into something immensely productive – life.

That's what this book has been about.

All you need is a little bit of hope. Hope to head back home into the unknown, like the prodigal son. Hope just to roll back the gravestone and see what Jesus does with what's inside.

Two scriptures have been the cornerstones of my personal resurrection. The first is Jeremiah 29:11: "'For I know the plans I have for you,' declares the Lord, 'plans to prosper you and not to harm you, plans to give you hope and a future.'" The other one is Romans 8:28: "And we know that in all things God works for the good of those who love him, who have been called according to his purpose."

These verses changed everything for me, because they gave me a hope that all the nonsense I've walked through will ultimately end up being used for God's glory. Further, they give us understanding that not all things are necessarily considered *good*. This is great news! This verse indicates that not everything is going to be good in your life. Struggles will come, brokenness will happen, and pain is unavoidable.

But here comes the hope: God also promises to work

it all together for His good. So God promises to work things together for His good, and in Jeremiah He promises us that He has plans to prosper us, to bring us out of places of exile, loneliness, depression, addiction, insecurity, doubt, or whatever plagues us.

Then we can have hope that never quits.

On the days when it gets rough, we've learned what to do. We have some tools in our tool belt to overcome the pain and fear that seeks to destroy. And if something happens and we do mess up, we fall back into something we shouldn't, please know this: God will not be disappointed.

His arms will always be open.

A relationship with God means He is always leaning in, pressing in, pursuing our souls, not with judgment, but always with love. God will not be alarmed by your mistakes nor will He love you any less.

The hope we cling to today that changes us is this: God loves you as much in your present situation as He did in the pain of your past.

When it comes to your life, God always gets the last word. And that last word is always going to bring hope. And hope changes everything.

ACKNOWLEDGMENT

To Adam Palmer: Thank you for helping to craft my voice and caring so much about other people that you would lend your incredible talent to someone like me. Because of you, countless people will find the hope they need to take the first step towards freedom. God is using you as the springboard, you as the match, and you as the catalyst to change lives. You are such a blessing to me and a gift to our world. I love you my friend and am excited to watch where God leads you in the years to come.

ABOUT THE AUTHOR

Lance Lang has devoted his life to inspiring hope in all those he comes across. His powerful story of overcoming addiction has touched the lives of thousands of people across the country. He is also the founder of Hope is Alive Ministries, a non-profit organization devoted to supporting men and women recovering from all types of addictions. Through this organization, Lance provides addiction outreach, prevention, and referral services to individuals, churches, and businesses. He is also a sought-after speaker, successful blogger, and marketing consultant.

Connect with Lance:

   @LanceLang   Lance@LanceLang.com

hope is alive
ministries

Hope is Alive Ministries (HIA) exists to do three things: Inspire Hope, Build Foundations and Change Lives. We accomplish these things through these three outlets:

- **Hope HQ** – A mentoring home for recovering addicts who are trying to turn their lives around. Men ready to take their recovery to the next level. Men who have decided they want everything they possibly can get from this life and are willing to work hard to achieve it. (Future homes opening soon in OKC and Tulsa)

- **Inspiring Events** – Several times throughout the year HIA hosts inspirational and informative events we call Nights of Hope. These engagingly creative events provide recovering addicts a place to celebrate their accomplishments while offering education and free resources to those actively affected by addiction.

- **Family Services** – Addiction isolates the family, leaving them feeling helpless, alone, and filled with shame. We strive to pull families back together and point them towards hope. HIA provides addiction outreach, prevention, and referral services to individuals and churches through our partnership program.

READ MORE ABOUT HOPE IS ALIVE MINISTRIES

www.HopeisAlive.net

Connect with HIA

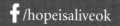 /hopeisaliveok    @Hope_is_Alive    @HopeisAliveOK